THE GREATEST OF THESE

THE WIT, WISDOM AND MEMORIES OF ASA DORSEY
A Georgia Mountains Holiness Preacher

Asa Dorsey

by Larry Fricks

"And now abideth faith, hope, charity, these three;
but the greatest of these is charity."

I Corinthians 13:13
King James Version of the Bible

Published in 2003 by
Fricks Publications
PO Box 492
Cleveland, Georgia 30528

2nd Edition Published in 2003

The Greatest of These
Copyright © 2003 by Larry Fricks

ISBN 0-9742411-0-5

Cover art: Annie Kate Dorsey, 1981
Back cover photo courtesy of Eunice and Nella Jones
Cover design: Andrew Miller, Lazer Age, Inc., Atlanta, Georgia
Book design: Stephanie Troncalli, Lazer Age, Inc., Atlanta, Georgia
Printed by Central Plains Book Manufacturing, Winfield, Kansas

COMMUNITY REFLECTIONS:

Asa Dorsey's name is as familiar to North Georgians as White County's Yonah Mountain, in whose shadow he preached, sawmilled, farmed and endeared himself to his beloved neighbors. In his book, he draws on his varied experiences to weave a story of how a struggling young country preacher persevered to become a revered man of the Gospel who continues to serve his God and his people after more than eight decades.

Johnny Vardeman, Managing editor (retired), *The Times*, Gainesville

If ever a man lived who was unselfish, uncomplicated, unassuming and unbiased in his love for others, it is Asa Dorsey. Rev. Dorsey is as open as the Good Book he has cradled for more than 80 years in his pursuit of God's will. If you read his delightful stories, you'll see his kindness and understand why he is one of the most cherished products of Northeast Georgia.

Phil Hudgins, Senior Editor, *Community Newspapers, Inc.*

"I'm grateful that it was part of God's plan that Asa Dorsey touched the families of White County and Northeast Georgia the way that he has. His life has enriched the lives of many other people, not only through his ministry, but also through his family. He has the absolute calling to know and say the right things that people need to hear at a special time. He's a remarkable man."

Carol Jackson, Georgia Senator

Annie Kate and Rev. Dorsey at their 50th wedding anniversary in 1986

DEDICATION

In memory of my life's mate, Annie Kate,
for all her love and support

Reverend Asa Dorsey

50th District State Sen. Carol Jackson, right, presents a resolution proclaiming "the Rev. Asa Dorsey Day" in Georgia to the Rev. Dorsey, center, and his daughter, Miriam Vandiver.

A RESOLUTION

Commending Reverend Asa Dorsey; and for other purposes.

WHEREAS, Reverend Asa Dorsey has followed the call to serve the mountain residents of northeast Georgia for the past 70 years; and

WHEREAS, whether the task is preparing a sermon, visiting the sick, counseling the troubled, baptizing a new believer, or any of the other countless responsibilities of a minister of the Gospel, Reverend Dorsey has shown the energy, devotion, and commitment truly reflective of divine guidance; and

WHEREAS, the unmatched spiritual assistance offered by Reverend Dorsey is a source of strength, inspiration, and direction for persons in all walks of life and from all economic strata; and

WHEREAS, it is abundantly fitting and proper for this body to recognize the outstanding accomplishments of the dynamic Christian ministry of this devout and pious man.

NOW, THEREFORE, BE IT RESOLVED BY THE SENATE that the members of this body commend Reverend Asa Dorsey for his unparalleled record of community service and his innumerable good works rendered on behalf of persons in need.

BE IT FURTHER RESOLVED that the Secretary of the Senate is authorized and directed to transmit an appropriate copy of this resolution to Reverend Asa Dorsey.

Senate Resolution 440
   By: Senator Jackson of the 50th

Adopted in the Senate April 17, 2003

PRESIDENT OF THE SENATE

SECRETARY OF THE SENATE

PRESIDENT PRO TEMPORE

SENATOR, DISTRICT 50th

Georgia Senate Resolution commending Rev. Dorsey. 2003

CONTENTS

FOREWORD, SECOND EDITION

I sensed that the extraordinary, grace-filled life of Rev. Asa Dorsey with his wisdom, humor and historic insights into old Appalachian ways would attract readers, but never imagined the first printing would sell out within 30 days. Thank you, members of the community, for your incredible support.

In this, the second edition, I have added at the end of the book an addendum, a story about a bear that broke into a federal post office. Enjoy it as you reflect on mountain life and an Appalachian view the world.

With deep appreciation,

Larry Fricks, Author and Publisher

INTRODUCTION BY LARRY FRICKS

I first experienced a funeral service by the Reverend Asa Dorsey after the 1988 passing of my Turner's Corner neighbor, Zora Jarrard. It had been a joy to be in the company of Zora, a woman who drew from a deep well of spiritual peace.

There was standing room only at the Welcome Holiness Church when Rev. Dorsey began his soothing stories about Zora's life and what she meant to family and friends. I could not recall hearing a minister with a more calm, nurturing voice, whose humble words radiated such profound compassion. His dignified reciting of scriptures from memory gave moral assurance that Zora had truly made her peaceful transition.

"I've seen when Asa Dorsey was preaching a funeral, he would shed tears, and there's not a lot of ministers that would do that," says my 85-year-old neighbor, Nora Gold. "He didn't preach just a lot of words, you could tell he really had compassion for the family."

Those unique oratory gifts combined with deep empathy offered comfort at some 1,700 funerals conducted by Rev. Dorsey throughout North Georgia and surrounding states. Many in the community say he has presided over more funerals than any other mountain preacher. But that's just part of what makes Rev. Dorsey an Appalachian legend. We hope this book will fill in some of the rest of the folklore.

During my career as a staff writer and columnist for local newspapers, we annually held "best in the community" write-in contests. Rev. Dorsey was consistently the people's pick for favorite minister. In fact even last year, at age 86, long retired from any pulpit, he still was voted the best. And this year, the Georgia Senate passed a resolution introduced by Senator Carol Jackson of White County recognizing the extraordinary fruits of Rev. Dorsey's 70-year ministry.

The call from Trilla Pruitt, Rev. Dorsey's daughter, inquiring whether I would consider publishing a book about the family patriarch, was an answer to hope. As an advocate for people with mental illness I had been working at the state mental health headquarters in Atlanta for nearly a decade, but longed for a return to writing, spending more time with my wife Grace at home, and reconnecting with our community in the mountains.

So I loaded a cassette tape in a recorder and headed over to Asa Dorsey Road in White County to begin capturing the experiences of a beloved, funeral-comforting Holiness preacher. What I discovered was much more. As a journalist I've interviewed thousands of people over the years, but I have never personally encountered anyone with such a remarkable memory for dates, details and reciting scriptures, all of which is rendered with a spellbinding gift for telling stories.

As Rev. Dorsey's words began flowing on to tapes, I realized we were recording a treasure of insights into the old Appalachian ways. Ways that included the critical role mountain religion – with its emotional revivals, camp meetings, faith healing and foot washings – played in socialization and the institution of community morals amid the demanding grind of agricultural life and struggles with poverty. Woven in the story of the Rev. Dorsey are insights into the wit, humor and fierce independence of Southern highlanders, such as Jack Turner and his mischievous buddies who dragged an ornery goat to a tent-meeting altar "to pray the devil" out of the stubborn creature. The unrepentant goat instead demolished the altar, mystifying the preachers who showed up later to lead the service.

There are great lessons in Rev. Dorsey's stories: the value of good neighbors; the experience of going broke; the faith and compassion hewed by repaying his creditors. There are wise words about marriages that stay together in tough times; the gift of a true soul mate and well-raised children. There are warnings about the hypocrisy of false prophets and churches that become misled by man-made rules; seductive promises of "prosperity theology"; and pride's abuse of spiritual gifts such as speaking in tongues. There are accounts of the work of angels and miracles.

Tommy Irvin, Georgia's Agriculture Commissioner, joins a host of friends and family who share their opinions on what sets the Rev. Dorsey apart from many who attempt to do God's work. Some recall memories of the attacks on the Holiness movement when it first came to these mountains, and how peace-seeking men and women like Rev. Dorsey won their enemies over by responding with love.

And then there's the reason the book is named *The Greatest of These* inspired by Rev. Dorsey's seven decades in ministry, and arriving at a truth that divine presence is evidenced best by charity as described in First Corinthians, chapter 13, verse 13. That insight helped strengthen Rev. Dorsey's commitment to welcome area hippies to his church during the tumultuous 1960s and '70s, when other churches were closing their doors to them, and questioning his support of the long-haired rebels.

All the chapters in the book except the last are the words of Rev. Dorsey, and family and friends, as recorded on tape. In the final chapter I attempted to capture how Holiness evangelism evolved from the 18th Century teachings of John Wesley and the Methodists into the present day Pentecostal movement that is sweeping over continents, especially third-world countries where poverty and hopelessness are rampant.

I pray in this book we color in at least some of the highlights of the remarkable journey of the Rev. Dorsey and his quiet, behind-the-scenes efforts as a one-man Red Cross. He has been a vessel for opening hearts, spreading peace and promoting values of charity among generations of mountain families.

I would like to thank three remarkable women who provided support in making this book a reality – former *Atlanta Magazine* staff writer Candice Dyer for her editing and Afterword; historian Shirley McDonald for securing pictures and filling in facts; and my wife Grace, who helps me believe I can.

1

RAISED UP AT MOSSY CREEK

I was borned September 22, 1915, into a rather large family.
There were four girls older than me which were: Marylou, Pearl,
Daisy and Mamie. Then the boys started coming along. There was
B.C., P.S., and then I was next, then John Carter and Clinton.
There were nine of us children borned to Albert Arnold and Annie
Alexander Dorsey.

My dad was the ninth generation from the original immigrant,
Major Edward Dorsey, that come from England and settled in
Maryland in 16 and 42. Major Dorsey built a home in Annapolis,
Maryland, and that home was the site of the first meetings of the
Provincial Government after Annapolis was established as the capi-
tal of the Province of Maryland in 1695. My mother was an
Alexander, the daughter of Thomas Watson Alexander, and he mar-
ried Rebecca Haynes.

My grandfather was Peyton Smith Dorsey, and he married
Temple Louise Henderson, that was from Shoal Creek in White
County. We were raised up in White County at Mossy Creek, and
my great-grandfather, John Major Dorsey, built the first cabin at
Mossy Creek Methodist Campground. His father, Andrew Dorsey,
helped organize Mossy Creek Methodist Campground in 1833, and
was one of the first trustees.

I was named for Asa G. Candler, a Bishop of the Methodist Church from Atlanta, and an owner of Coke. We come from a long line of Methodists, but I changed that.

I was borned at home in the old Woodlawn School building my dad bought for us in 1906 to live in. Doc Evans delivered me. One of Doc Evans' grandson's – Phillip Hunt – is still living over here near me. E. B. Hunt, who had the store nearby was also Doc Evans' grandson.

The old Woodlawn School was located near what is now the intersection of Lotheridge and Asa Dorsey Road. The building was 40 feet wide and 60 feet long, and it didn't have a partition in it. We all lived in that big open area. We had a bed in every corner. We pulled in an old No. 2 wash tub once a week and heated water on the cook stove and poured it in there. We used the old Octagon Soap, which was a nickel a bar.

Dad went to school there in the late 1800s. He said they had just one teacher for the whole school, grades one through seven. The teacher's last name was Quinlan. When the students would do something wrong, during the recess the teacher would take them down to a branch in heavy woods below the schoolhouse. They'd be gone maybe 15 or 20 minutes and dad said no student would ever tell what happened, but they never had to go a second time.

The school building was made of dressed-by-hand pine heart lumber. The boards were about 12 inches wide and the roof was made of white oak boards. When it would snow in the wintertime, we'd wake up and there'd be an inch of snow on our covers. The walls didn't have insulation and the snow would come in through the cracks. We had an outhouse about 50 yards from the house. There was just one acre with the schoolhouse, but on the other side of the road dad owned 60 acres.

When I was 15, and my brother P.S. was 17, we bought lumber

and run a partition halfway cross the house. Then we run another partition halfway on the south end of the house, which was 20 feet on each side, and made a dining room out of one and a bedroom out of the other. They lived there until 19 and 44 when my dad built the white house that still faces on Lotheridge Road near the intersection of Asa Dorsey Road. I remember my dad took the Atlanta Constitution, and he kept up with World War I.

I guess my earliest recollection of the mountains was about my dad. Back then we got fertilizer in 200-pound bags. Sometimes the bags were made of burlap; sometimes they'd be cotton. Dad would take those burlap bags, and in the fall we'd get in the wagon and go up to Yonah peak. We'd pick that bag full of chestnuts off the ground and bring them back home. We'd have roasted chestnuts for months. We roasted them over a fire inside our home. The taste of those chestnuts was much different from the Chinese chestnuts we have today. Those chestnut trees were huge trees. They cut them for years, and split them, and made chestnut fence rails.

Another of my earliest remembrances was the old Northwestern Railroad that run up through White County, and went on to Helen because of the Morse Brothers Lumber Company in Helen. They were a big sawmill. Dad took me up there to see one of the sawmills. There was a big building with a sawmill on each side and they was powered by steam. They had a band saw, not a circle saw. There were four men on the carriage. One stood at each head block and had on a big wide belt that was fastened by another leather belt to a head block. When that carriage would start you could imagine how steam would start it with such a jerk. It would have knocked them off, if they hadn't been buckled to the head block.

I was so amazed at the size of those logs. I was hardly five years old then, but I remember there were logs as wide as I was tall. Some of those trees were standing, no doubt, when America was discovered – those big yellow poplars. They'd saw some of those big logs into 18-inch boards, 16 feet long. They had a train that run from Helen all back through the mountains, even as far over as Turner's Corner. They'd cut out all the virgin timber back in those mountains. We'd go over to where the railroad came in with a load of logs. They'd pump water out of the river and make a big pond between the mill and the river. They'd dump those logs into that pond, and then they had men with rubber suits on up to their waist. Their feet were covered in that rubber, and they'd be up on those logs, with what looked like a hoe handle with a sharp thing. They'd stick that in one of the logs and start pushing it. There was a big chain that come down out of each sawmill, and that chain would catch those logs.

After the lumber was sawed it was stacked all down through those river bottoms, even down to the curve where Mr. Vandiver lived on the hill. They had tracks that ran all the way through there, and they had little trolleys that they stacked their lumber on. Even though they had a dry kiln, they would dry it a while before they dry-kilned it. They sawed one hundred thousand feet of lumber a day there. They kept busy with all the carloads of lumber going by train from Helen to the market.

There was a bunch of men back in those valleys living in tents. I talked with Jonah Thomas. He was one of the men that pulled one end of those seven-foot crosscut saws. He said they would go up on the side of those mountains and cut that big timber. There would be logging roads they logged on with horses. They would build those roads so the horses could go up there and pull the logs out.

The Northwestern Railroad run a freight train and a passenger train in White County. When it left Gainesville it had three stops to make before it got to Helen: Clermont; Mel Dean's, a depot that was near U.S. 129 and Westmoreland Road; and then Cleveland. My aunt would come up every spring from Florida. She'd change trains in Gainesville, from Southern to Northwestern, and we'd have to take our wagon to meet her over at Mel Dean's station.

I rode with my dad in the wagon when I was just seven or eight years old, and the first car I remember seeing in White County belonged to Frank Carrol, our mailman. My dad and myself would drive mules. When we'd meet that Model T Ford, those mules would almost run away with him. They were so scared of that moving vehicle. I always dreaded meeting that car because the mules had such a fit.

I remember, I must have been ten years old, when dad loaded us up in the wagon early one Sunday morning and pulled out for Yonah Mountain. We went around on the other side of the mountain and come in at the old ginseng farm, which was up on the side of Pink Mountain. We left our mules and wagons down in the big apple orchard at the foot of Pink. We'd walk up to the ginseng farm where the man had crossties filled with dirt, and the ginseng growing in that. He shipped most of his ginseng to Europe, where they'd pay a high price for ginseng. There was a path that led from that ginseng farm up one of the ridges, and wound around and come in on the south side of Lover's Leap. I remember going there, and dad showed us how to pull our handkerchiefs out and throw them off of Lover's Leap. In a few minutes, the handkerchiefs would come floating back up. That amazed me.

They had what they called a "tight squeeze" there. It was two rocks that stood up about 20 feet and there was just a narrow place between them. We'd go down and go through that tight squeeze. My dad was a pretty heavy man; he weighed nearly 200 pounds. He sort of got wedged in there one day.

Just below the tight squeeze they had what was called the

"Devil's Pulpit." Us boys, we decided to go in that Devil's Pulpit. It had a hole in the rock, and it was dark as midnight in there. There was rocks you had to crawl over that bruised your knees, and I remember you could just imagine feeling those snakes.

When I was growing up we didn't have any toys to play with. So dad bought a new wheelbarrow, and we wore it out running it 'round and 'round in the yard. Then dad built a shop down below his house. His brother-in-law, Calvin Hulsey, was a good black-smith. He come down there to dad's shop and started working at rebuilding some wagon wheels. The Piedmont wagon had a big wooden hub that supported the spokes that went up to the rim, where the steel band was around the top. The Bagwell wagon, made in Gainesville, had an iron hub. Us boys, we'd take those iron hubs that went up against the axle, and we'd turn them around. Then we'd drive them together, and it would make a big iron spool. We'd go to the woods and cut down a stick that had a fork in it, and we'd start pushing those hubs around over the yard, and make a bad place in the yard.

My sisters were older than us boys, and they kept those yards clean by going into the woods and cutting Dogwood brooms and tying them together. They swept those yards every Saturday. A sprig of grass wasn't allowed to grow because back then grass had no place in the yard; they had to be smooth and clean. Our sisters would really fuss at us for making those rows in the yard.

On Sunday afternoon there was nothing to do, so we'd all get together and play games. We were joined by T.B. Hooper's son, Mel Dean; Ben Trotter's sons, Hobart and Travis; and the Craven boys, Leonard and Robert.

One game we played was called "Pine Needle Fox." Back in those days, for Christmas, some of us boys would get a capbuster pistol. We'd get a roll of caps with it, and they were great gifts.

We'd appoint one of the boys to be the man, and he was given a capbuster pistol with some caps in it. Then we would choose two boys to be the foxes. They'd start out through the woods, breaking off pine limbs just six or eight inches long, and dropping them about every 50 yards. That's why we called it "Pine Needle Fox." The other boys, except the one chosen to be the man, they were called the dogs. After about 30 minutes, the man would start the dogs on the trail of the two foxes. They'd come through the woods, and find those pine needles, and that's the way they tracked the fox. Of course the fox would climb a few feet up that tree. The man would come with his capbuster, and he'd fire, and one of the boys would jump out. Then he'd fire at the other one, and he'd jump out. That was the game we played.

Then we had another very dangerous game we played called "Kack." In that game we'd get in the big woods below where my house is built now. At that time it was a big forest full of big trees. We'd climb to the top of those trees, and get to swinging back and forth enough until we could catch on to a limb of the adjoining tree, and swing over onto it. The one that could stay in the trees the longest was the champion. When I look back on that game now, I think about how dangerous that was, because we was in the tops of trees and we could have easily fallen and got a neck broke.

I remember the Craven boys' father, Ed Craven, had a topless buggy. When we would catch Mr. Craven gone – and he'd be gone for a little bit – we'd get his buggy and take the shafts out. His son, Robert, which was the youngest, he'd get one of his dad's plow lines and tie it to the left side of the axle of the buggy, and the other to the right side. Then he would set in the floorboard with his feet propped up against the dash, and that's how he would guide the buggy.

This hill, that's still here near my house, it would be a job to pull the buggy up this long hill, but we'd get it to the top. At the top we'd turn it around and Robert would take his position in the floor-board, wrap the plow lines around his left and right hands where he could guide it. P.S. and myself, we'd be the ones that would push off, and we'd get going as fast as we could run without falling down. Then we'd reach up and catch the back of the buggy and pull ourselves up on the back axle. We'd stand on the back axle and there'd be two or three boys inside the buggy. Robert was setting on the floorboard and we'd pick up a good bit of speed going down this hill. We'd always grease the buggy good so it would roll easy on the axles.

Two roads come together below where Leonard Craven built his new house. There was a hill down to the creek there. One Sunday we'd got Mr. Craven's buggy and taken the ride of our life. We come down that hill and Robert was singing the train wreck song, "Old 97."

Just as we got to the bridge, here come Doc. Elrod in a T Model. We just knew we were going to get hurt. But Robert jerked that buggy into what he thought was the creek. Before we got to the bridge, there was a grapevine, about as big as your arm. It happened to be swinging there anchored up in a tree. When that buggy hit the vine it got caught in it, and swung out over the water with enough momentum to swing us back onto the bank. That was our last buggy ride.

When I was younger I went to school down at Woodlawn old school and we played basketball. We'd play different schools like Shoal Creek, and Steep Hollow over in Habersham on Duncan Bridge Road. One day we played Demorest, and those boys come dressed in basketball attire, and they had on tennis shoes. I remember Gordan Hicks, he was the forward man. They'd get the ball to him and he could really run. They appointed me the running guard, so it was my position to guard Gordan to keep the ball away from him. But he could run a little faster than I could. We were playing on dirt. Well, it was fine gravel. We was going down the court and I was trying to keep up with Gordan, but I seen he was going to get to the goal. I just hung an old brogan that I had on in his pants leg and tripped him, but he fell on me. His knee hit me in my left side and I didn't know it, but it ruptured me at the time.

In the next few days a knot come out there, but I didn't say nothing about it. Then it got so sore I mentioned it to my mother. My sister, Daisy, had married Doc. Bulgin's son, George, and Doc lived with them. Daisy happened to come that evening, and mother told them that I had a knot on my side that the doctor needed to look at. So I went home with them.

The doctor come in and he looked at that knot and he said, "Oh, he got a rupture I'll have to fix."

So he got my brother-in-law to get up on the bed with me, and put his knees on each of my arms, to where I couldn't move. He took his fingers and worked that knot out. I thought I'd faint. He got my entrails back in the right place and taped me up so tight I couldn't hardly breathe. I had to lay on my back for two or three weeks. I was about 12 years old then; it was in the summer, and they brought me home and put me to bed. I was just in the fourth grade, and I never went back to school. I graduated in the fourth grade.

Our neighbor, T.B. Hooper, had a pretty good-sized apple orchard pretty close to the top of Skitts Mountain, on the northeast side. He had a big pair of horses and a big wagon; those horses would pull that wagon up Skitts. Mr. Hooper would work his apple trees and spray them. He had some of the best apples, and us boys and dad would go there after Christmas. He grew some Terry apples; I haven't seen any of those in years. They'd just begin to get good along after Christmas. After we'd talk a while, he'd pick up his bucket, and we was always glad to see him go to the apple house. He'd come back with the bucket about half full, and we would eat apples to our fill.

My brother-in-law, Clarence Simmons, was a mechanic. He worked for J.B.R. Barrett that owned the Ford dealership in Cleveland. Clarence married my oldest sister, Marylou. They bought ten acres of land adjoining my dad's farm and built a small house on it. Clarence bought an old T model. Back then it was fun to take an old car that was about used up and make a strip down out of it. You took the fenders, the hood and other covers off it until all you had left was the radiator, the engine, the dash, the gas tank and the wheels. You sat on the gas tank and drove the car.

I was just 12 years old then and I thought, "I'd like to have Clarence's strip down."

I had a shotgun that I had traded a dog for to my neighbor. I thought a lot of my shotgun because I was an avid hunter back in my early days. This was a Baystake single-barrel shotgun, 32-inch barrel, full choke. I killed a lot of rabbits with that gun. My neighbor, when he ordered it in 19 and 24 from Sears and Roebuck, he gave eight dollars and 95 cents for it. I traded him my dog for it.

I went over to my brother-in-law's one day and we was looking at his strip down and I thought it would be fun to have it.

I told Clarence, "I'll give you my shotgun for your strip down."

Clarence was a World War I veteran, and he was a good shot.

He said, "Well, I'll have to try your gun out."

I just had one shell left so I suggested, "We'll have to go down to Uncle Henry Alexander's store and buy some shells."

We were walking down the road, and we got about 200 yards from the store. One of my brothers was walking with us and he looked up and saw a hawk sailing way up high and said, "Look, there's a hawk!"

Back then we killed every hawk that come around because they killed our baby chicks. If the old hens could raise their baby chicks that hatched they'd be our fryers to eat in the spring and summer. The hawks was bad to swoop down and pick up one of the young chicks, so we kept our guns ready to kill the hawks.

Clarence looked up and said, "If you can kill that hawk with that gun I'll give you the strip down for the gun."

I was a crack shot even at that age. I had one shotgun shell. I lifted that gun up and when I pulled the trigger that hawk come tumbling down. My brother-in-law stuck to his word; he gave me the old strip down for the shotgun. Us boys had a time playing with that old strip down. Of course, you couldn't drive it on muddy roads; it would cover you up with mud.

One day, when I was about 13, I went with my dad down to Uncle Bill Hulsey's corn mill. We had to go to the corn mill about every two weeks with two bushels of corn. There was nine in my family, and it took a lot of corn meal to make our cornbread. I called Uncle Billy "uncle" because one of his sons married my dad's sister. I just always called him "Uncle Billy" and his wife "Aunt Josie." We went to the mill that day and Uncle Billy, he'd bought him a T Model, about a 19 and 25. It was a touring car. That is, it didn't have any sides; it just had a top to it.

Uncle Billy asked, "Arnold, can that boy of yours drive an old car?"

I guess because I had that old strip down my dad answered, "Pshaw Billy, he can drive anything."

Uncle Billy said, "Well Arnold, you look after the mill while the boy and me goes over to Bill Pressley's store to get some stuff we need."

I had never drove a real car before, only that strip down. Of course, you had to crank a T Model with a hand crank. I got the switch turned on. Those old T Models had a rod come up on each side of the steering wheel. Then they made a 90-degree turn just under the steering wheel and the ends of the rods was flattened out to where you could just slip them between your fingers and work them. The right rod was your gas and the left rod was your spark. You had a set of coils that sat under the dashboard that furnished the spark for the car to run on. If you happened to forget and leave the spark pulled down too far, that car, when you went to crank it, would kick so hard a lot of people got their arms broke with those old T Models.

Those old touring cars didn't have a door on the driver's side up front. They had a back door on each side, but the front just had the one door on the passenger side. You had to climb over about a two-foot high sidewall on the driver's side.

I finally got the car cranked and got in and killed the motor the first thing. I had to crawl out again and get the car cranked. That time I got started with it and the further we went the more I liked to drive that thing. We went up to the store and Uncle Billy put gas in it and then bought some groceries. We drove back, and I just parked the car outside of his car shed. He'd built a new car shed for that car right on the edge of the creek. The back of the shed was almost on the bank of the creek.

So I left the car parked outside the shed. That evening, Uncle Billy decided he'd put his car up. He got it cranked and got in it. He got his car in the shed, but he forgot to take his foot off the pedal for the low gear. Uncle Billy drove that car through the shed and plunged off into the creek with it.

Aunt Josie come out screaming and hollering.

He said, "Hush Josie, it ain't nothing but an old car in the creek!"

That ended Uncle Billy's driving.

Doc Evans was our doctor and he traveled by horse and buggy.

They didn't have no phones, so you'd have to go get the doctor if you needed him. He didn't have no office for patients to come to; he had to come to the homes. He would come any time of the day or night that you called him. When I was just eight or nine years old my dad took typhoid fever. Several people died with typhoid. Doc Evans come and doctored my dad through that typhoid, and he was well in about six weeks.

C.H. Freeman and John Kenimer owned the largest country store in White County. At that time, the Leaf community had a post office that was located in that store and there was a mail route from it. Mr. Freeman had his office for the postal service in the northeast side of the building. On the west side of the store, about 20 feet from his office, stood a big, old pot-bellied stove about shoulder-high. Since he had to work in that office he kept that stove, in cold weather, full of wood and real good and hot.

There come in a salesman one day from Gainesville, before there were heaters in all the cars. He had on a big overcoat, but he come in and said, "I'm chilled."

The salesman stood by that big stove a little bit, and then he said to Mr. Freeman, "I've got the toothache so bad I just can't hardly go."

Mr. Freeman was an old original historian and a steward in the Methodist Church at Zion as long as it had services. He and I had become great friends.

He said to the salesman, "Well, I do say now, I've got the very remedy."

At the end of the counter on the southside of the store he had a little glass showcase that he called his "notion counter." In it he had all home remedies and such you could buy without a prescription. He reached in there and got a bottle about as big as your thumb. It had a dropper in it.

He said to the salesman, "Now, I do say now, dab a little of this on that tooth."

So the salesman just took him at his word, opened the bottle and got a little in the dropper. Then he put a drop on the back tooth that was hurting him.

Then he put the dropper back in the bottle and handed it to Mr. Freeman who returned it to the notion case.

After a few minutes the salesman reached in his mouth and began to pull out some stripping.

He asked, "Mr. Freeman, what was that you gave me to go on my tooth?"

Mr. Freeman responded, "I do say now, that was Upjohn's toothache drops, or I thought it was."

He come back and reached in and got the bottle and held it up and said, "Well, now I do say, that's Blue Jay Corn Remover."

The salesman said, "Well it's playing havoc with the stripping on my jaw, but that tooth hasn't hurt a lick since that drop hit it."

When I was 14 and 15 I started playing baseball over in what we called the Carter bottoms. My dad had rented the Carter place. We farmed part of it, and part was left for pasture, a big pasture. So we would meet on Saturday and we organized what we called the White Creek Baseball Team. We played Cleveland and other teams around. I played different positions. I was hind catcher for a while, then I started pitching some. After I started pitching, my brother, P.S., he was on the team so he would catch with me at home. We would get in from the fields at dinner, as soon as we could eat a bite, we'd go out to pitch some. I had me a piece of plank cut the same size as the plate. I'd get P.S. to stand behind that homemade plate, and I'd pitch to him. He'd do all right 'til I got warmed up. At this time I was 15 and weighed about 160 pounds, and I had quite a bit of strength. So I would give him one of my fastballs and it would sting him through his glove. He'd jump up and throw his mitt at me, and he'd go into the house.

After I was saved, they condemned ball games, picture shows and all worldliness, so that ended my ball playing.

Many times we would just go up on the mountains. I loved the view that you could see from the top of Yonah, Skitts and Pink mountains. The mountains have always been an attraction for me. In later years, my son Phillip would rent us houses on the beach and we'd go to the beach, and sometimes stay a week, sometimes two weeks. But I'd tell the family I'd rather be home looking at these mountains. That's one reason why I went to great trouble to clear out the woods below my house where I live now, to bring Yonah and Pink in view from my patio here. Everyday I look at those two mountains.

2

MOUNTAIN FARMING AND THE GREAT DEPRESSION

I remember in 19 and 25, before the child labor law, I'd just had my tenth birthday; dad had a '25 model Dodge screened in truck. Apple picking time come at Yonah Fruit Company, and dad went over and got a bunch of jobs for several men. He asked me, P.S. and B.C. to work, too. They let me and P.S. work climbing those apple trees, getting those apples the fellas on the ground couldn't reach. I made 50 cents a day, and to me that was good money. On Friday, for five days' work, I'd get my check for two dollars and a half. That was a little strange to me, to have any money at my age.

As I grew up, my father learned us to do a lot of things. I was plowing a mule in the fields by the time I was 11 years old. I remember when spring came dad would plant about 10 to 12 acres in cotton. Cotton was our money crop. Then he'd plant 20 to 25 acres in corn. Corn was our bread that we ate, mainly cornbread. Of course we had the flour that mother cooked biscuits for breakfast with. Many times it was homemade flour where dad had grown the wheat, taken it to the wheat mill, and had flour made out of it.

We'd also use corn to fatten our hogs and feed our mules on.

We'd feed each mule six ears of corn every morning and a bundle of fodder. At dinner, and at night, we'd give them the same thing. It took quite a bit of corn to go through the winter.

When spring would come, at planting time, dad would plow with a two-horse turner. He had a drag harrow he made out of wood in a v-shape and drove pieces of rod down in it. Then he'd turn that over, and he'd run that over the plowed field, and it would sort of smooth it off. Then he'd lay it off in rows.

I sort of hated the job, but we'd fertilize our corn with stable manure from where the mules had stayed all winter. We had quite a bit of manure from the mules and the cows. We'd pull the wagon next to the door of the stable. Two men in the stable with pitch-forks would fork up that manure and throw it out on the wagon. A man on the wagon with a hoe busted those big clods of manure up. Finally, we'd get that wagon bed full of that stable manure, and then we'd carry it out to the fields.

Dad would already have the rows laid off. We planted our corn then in three-foot wide rows. Each hill was 36 inches apart. We'd take our fertilizer bags, the 200-pound bags, and rip them open to make aprons out of them. We'd tie those aprons around our waist, tie them in the back, with them hanging down below our knees. When we got to the field one fella would stay on the wagon with a shovel and the others put on their aprons and catch up each corner of the apron that was hanging down. We'd hold it up to make a sack-like. The fella on the wagon would fill our aprons full of that manure; it was heavy.

We'd go down the row that was laid off. We had to estimate the distance of about three feet, then we'd raise that apron up and lower it down 'til where we could shake it a little. About two hand-fuls would come out to a hill. And that's the way we fertilized the corn. It was one of the hardest jobs I had as a younger boy.

As I grew up, my dad had an old grain cradle that was made out of white ash, which was the lightest, hard wood there was. When I was just seven or eight years old I remember going up to Silas Cantrell's. Silas lived two or three miles above us. He was a cradle maker. He'd go into the swamps around here and harvest white ash and use that wood to make cradles. When Silas made a cradle it just weighed seven or eight pounds. When you bought the cradles that were manufactured, they'd weigh 14 to 15 pounds.

The cradle had about a five-foot blade on it called a scythe, and above the blade it had five fingers. It had a big handle that come up with a big crook and we'd slip a handle down to about a man's height. And we'd tighten that up to where we could lift the weight of that cradle with our right hand, and our left hand we used to swing back and forth and go through the grain. The grain would fall on the fingers, and when we'd make a sweep, we'd have to hold the cradle up against our hip and gather the grain off and put it in a pile. That was man's work, but I started doing that when I was about 14. I got so good at cutting grain with dad's cradle 'til our neighbors began to hire me to cut their grain.

The grain would be cut in June. Those hot days in June we'd swing that cradle 'til I'd get so wet with perspiration that it'd feel like needles sticking in my back. But I'd keep swinging that cradle. If you could cut a hundred shock of grain a day, you was doing a fair job with a cradle. A shock was ten bundles. There'd be tiers that come in behind me and they'd tie up a bundle of wheat, or rye, or oats, whatever it was, and throw it down. There would be maybe two others coming behind me, gathering eight bundles and standing them with the head up, leaning against one another; then taking two bundles with head down and spreading head open, one on either side covering the other eight; then tying the two bundles together. That shielded the grain from the rain. I got good with that cradle to where I could cut 200 shocks a day. And because I was using a cradle made by Silas Cantrell out of light white ash, I could stay ahead of most the cradlers in a big field. I had a cradle that was not hard to swing. I think the most I was ever paid was a dollar a day.

After I got married, dad kept that old cradle in what we called a shuck house, up in the rafters. It just laid up there. After mother passed away in '73, we had a sale. Everything sold, and I purchased that old cradle and brought it here because it meant so much to me. I got to thinking one day it would be good to give Bradley the cradle and let him hang it up over at Fonda Milling Company for show. The idea pleased Bradley; he hung the cradle in a back room that had a lot of activity. When the mill burned in March of '97 that was the end of the cradle.

Dad also taught me how to hew logs. Back then we had log-raisings. A man would come through on a mule – after he'd get his logs cut and drug up to the barn site where he wanted to build – and he'd announce having a log raising on a certain day. There'd be at least 10 or 12 men gather in for that log raising. They'd put one man with a sharp axe on each corner. They'd start off with hewing the sides, drop back about eight inches from the end, and sort of cut a "v" in that log for six or eight inches. Then when they'd put a cross log on it, we had to cut a notch in it to fit the "v." If it didn't fit right you'd turn it back up and hew a little more. By the time I was 15, I was bringing up a corner on one of those log buildings. There's a log barn still standing near my neighbor's house that was the last log-raising I ever attended, and I brought up the northwest corner of that barn.

Another memory of my childhood was the cotton picking and corn shucking we'd have. When fall would come we'd get our cotton picked. I always was a pretty good cotton picker. If you could pick 100 pounds a day you did good. Some days I could get 200 pounds. You got a dollar a 100 pounds for picking cotton for other people. Of course picking our own, we didn't get nothing.

After we got our cotton picked, we'd get together for a corn shucking. After several frosts and the cornstalk got brittle 'til where you could break the ear of corn off from the stalk good, we'd bring the corn to the house. We had a shed on each side of the corncrib. I guess the crib was about six feet wide. We had an a-frame to cover it. We'd throw that corn on the ground next to the crib. Off of the 25 acres, if we got 200 bushel, we were doing good. Nowadays, on a couple of acres people make 200 bushel, but back then we didn't farm like they do today. After we got our corn gathered, one of us would get on a mule and go through the community, announcing a corn shucking at Arnold Dorsey's this evening beginning at four o'clock.

It would be surprising the crowd that would come to a corn shucking. The men that come always brought their wives, and the wives would help mother fix a big supper for everybody. We'd shuck corn. When we got the shuck off of it, we'd put the shuck behind us, and throw the corn over in the crib. When anybody shucked a red ear of corn among the young people, they got to kiss anyone of their choosing. There was only two or three of red ears in the 200 bushels of corn, so everyone wanted to get that red ear.

The shucks would pile up and us young fellows, it was our job mostly, we'd lock our arms and join together and start kicking those shucks into a shed we had there until we filled the shed full. The last corn was shucked maybe by nine o'clock at night. We'd hang up lanterns for light. Then the men would help us, some of them would just gather the shucks up in their arms and take them to the shed. We'd fill up a pretty big shed full of shucks and we'd feed them to our cows during the winter. The cows really loved them shucks.

Then after the corn shucking there'd be several young people there, and they'd invite them in the house, and start playing games, all different kinds. A lot of people, when they had a corn shucking and when the shucking was over, would have a square dance. But we'd just let the young people play games for an hour or so before they went home.

At Mel Dean's train depot, near where Doc Evans lived, our neighbor T.B. Hooper was a fertilizer dealer, and he'd unload a carload of fertilizer he ordered. We'd go over in our wagon and get ten bags. The bags weighed 200 pounds, and that was something for us boys to do after we got bigger, was to show out shouldering those 200-pound bags of fertilizer. We'd load on ten bags, which was a ton, and that made it pretty heavy on a team of mules coming through the muddy roads. Sometimes the mud in places would be up to the axles on the wagons and the mules would have a time pulling the wagon through it. We'd use 20 to 25 bags of fertilizer in a year.

Most of the time they used burlap for those fertilizer bags, but sometimes they'd use cotton. We was always glad to see the cotton bags because we could cut them open, down each side and across the end, and make two towels out of a bag. They were a little rough to begin with for drying off, but as they got washed, they got softer. My mother, when she got enough, would take those cotton sacks, rip them open and make bed sheets out them. They would last and last.

My dad bought a 19 and 23 new Dodge truck, a screen in truck, from C.V. Nalley. I was just eight years old then. My dad wanted to get into buying and selling poultry. He bought him some chicken coops and put them in the back of that truck.

But dad couldn't drive. They explained to him how to drive, so dad went out one morning to try to drive. He kept his new truck in a shed. After he got the truck cranked and got it in reverse he come out of that shed pretty good. But he forgot how to stop it. We had a barn about 75 yards behind the shed, and dad backed into that barn in reverse and it bounced the truck forward. Then he hit the barn again and bounced back and did that 'til he killed his motor. That was the end of my dad's driving.

One of the first T Models that come into White County belonged to Hamp Autrey. Hamp was a blacksmith over this side of Mossy Creek Church. He had several boys. One of his boys, Toy, that was about 16 or 17 years old then, loved to drive that T Model. So dad went over and talked to Hamp about getting Toy to come live with us and drive dad's truck. He come and he was a good driver.

Back then, when we needed something from the store – sugar or soap or soda or lamp oil – we'd just run down a fryer or two, take it to the store, and swap it for what we needed. They would weigh the chicken and pay us by the pound. The store had a little pen to put their poultry in, the hens and the broilers. Dad would go around to those stores and buy their poultry.

They had a 50-pound lard tub, every store did, that had a lid on it. Back then every family had a cow and some of them had two. They'd make more butter than they could use, so they'd take the extra butter to the store and sell it. That merchant would just dump it in that tub. When the tub was full, dad would buy it, then he'd take a load of butter and poultry to Gainesville. He'd go to Brenau College and they'd buy a bunch of it. Then he'd go to the Dixie Hunt Hotel and the Princeton Hotel and they'd buy some. If he had any left over he'd go down to Mrs. Loudermilk's. Mrs. Loudermilk first married J.D. Jewell's father that passed away, then she remarried a Loudermilk.

Mr. Loudermilk had a big warehouse in Gainesville and dad would go over there. J.D. Jewell was just a young man at that time, but he'd built him some batteries back in the back of that warehouse to hold chickens in. He'd buy dad's poultry and put them in those batteries and feed them corn-meal dough 'til he got them real fat. Then J.D. would go the Princeton and Dixie Hunt Hotel to see how many dressed fryers they could use. He cut their heads off and dressed them and delivered them. That's the way J.D. Jewell got started in the poultry business. After he got married he started hatching a few chickens. He put out 250 baby chicks to a farm. They just had little buildings. They'd put the chicks in, heat it up with lanterns and they kept the chicken houses closed up. They just kept spreading out and they got to building bigger houses and by 19 and 40 they were building houses that would hold 1,000 to 1,500 chickens. They kept growing 'til 19 and 50 when some of them would build houses that would hold 2,000 to 2,500 chickens.

In front of that big warehouse in Gainesville was a fella that was a cotton buyer named Ralph Cleveland. He later owned and operated Gainesville Milling Company. We'd take our cotton down in a wagon. They'd have two or three of us boys get in the wagon and ride to Gainesville sitting on a couple of bales of cotton. Ralph would get up on the wagon, rip one side of that bale open, and pull out some cotton to decide how long the staple was. Then he'd go to the other side and rip it open. Some people would have some bad cotton so he'd check it in two or three places, then they'd unload it and put it in the warehouse.

When we'd go to Gainesville in a wagon it would take all day, about eight hours, to get there. It would be late in the evening and we'd put up the mules and stay in Bells Wagon Yard that was back behind where St. Paul's Methodist Church is. We paid $1.50 for use of the wagonyard overnight where there was a stall for the mules and a loft filled with hay above to spread our quilts and sleep. Dad would carry a head of cabbage with him, and some fatback meat that he had in the smokehouse, and some corn meal. They had a kitchen at the wagon yard with pans and skillets and you cooked in a fireplace. Dad would slit up that fatback, put it in a skillet to cook, and it would just be swimming in grease. He'd take the fatback out and leave the grease. He'd use his pocketknife to slit up the cabbage and drop it in the hot grease to cook. Then he'd take the cabbage out and make him up some cornmeal dough with a spoon. He'd pour that cornmeal dough into that skillet with all that grease and it would have some of the thickest crust. We loved that cornbread. That would be our supper.

Then for breakfast he'd use that fatback and he'd have a little flour with it, and a little syrup and some butter. He'd fry the side meat, then he'd make up the flour with a spoon and he'd pour it in the grease. It would make some of the best fritters you'd ever eat.

Back then folks would move to Gainesville to work in the cotton mill. They'd have families back in White County and would correspond by writing. They'd ask their family to bring them a milk cow. They'd just tie the cow behind the wagon and walk her all the way down to Gainesville to deliver the cow to the family.

The Great Depression come on. We called it, us farmers did, the "Hoover days" because Herbert Hoover was elected President. My dad and L.H. Alexander, my mother's first cousin, ran a store together in a store building that L.H. Alexander built in about 18 and 87. They deposited their money from the store in the Farmers and Merchants Bank in Cleveland. There were two banks in Cleveland at that time, the White County Bank and the Farmers and Merchants Bank. I remember going to the bank with my dad. In those Hoover days both of those banks had to close; they went broke. My dad owned some stock in the Farmers and Merchants

Bank, and he not only lost the money he had in that bank, he had
to give up the amount of the stock he had. Fortunately, we lived on a
farm where we grew most of what we eat, the vegetables and the meat.

We planted syrup cane to make syrup out of. Dad was a good
syrup maker. Every fall we would make syrup for ourselves, and
the community. Back then, syrup sold for 50 cents a gallon. But
very few people were buying anything in those days. Cotton got
down to about five cents a pound; a 500-pound bale of cotton
would only bring 25 dollars. My dad had an old phonograph and
he had a record with the words, "Five-cent cotton and 40-cent
meat, how in the world can a poor man eat?" I've never forgotten
that song.

When prices was high back in 1924 and 25, cotton got up to 40
cents a pound. We had a neighbor that wanted to sell his bale of
cotton but said he was going to hold out for 50 cents a pound.
Then it come down to five cents a pound. He just let it set out to
rot, he never did sell it. Those were hard days. We had to sow our
wheat and have the grain thrashed and get the bags of wheat. We
had to haul it to the wheat mill and have flour made out of it to use
for making biscuits for breakfast. Otherwise we'd have to fry cornbread fritters to eat with our white gravy and buttered syrup.

Sometimes, especially in the fall of the year and on into the late
winter, we'd have side meat. We'd have some ham and shoulder
meat from the hogs dad would kill and salt down in the smoke
house. But that wouldn't last a big family long, so we'd give out of
that meat to go with our white gravy. Of course we couldn't afford
to eat our eggs because those eggs, back during the Depression, was
sometimes dropped down to 50 cents a dozen, but most of the time
they was 60 cents, which was five cents an egg. We could take a
couple of eggs to the store and get a box of matches and a box of
soda. If we had three eggs we could get a gallon of kerosene oil for

our lamps. So we couldn't afford to eat our eggs the hens laid.

The hens would go to setting in the spring; mother would put the eggs under them and they'd hatch off a bunch of what we called biddies back then. Mother would grow those biddies up and they'd become fryers. Back then we'd just feed the chickens corn, shelled corn, and they'd get pretty fat in 14 or 15 weeks. We'd go out some mornings and run down a fryer. Mother would dress it. Of course us men would have to take it to the chopping block with a sharp axe and cut its head off. When it bled real good we'd bring it to mother and she'd have a kettle of scalding water. She'd put that fryer in a dishpan and pour that scalding water over it. That made it so those feathers would almost fall out. There was a bunch of fuzz like on the skin under the feathers. She'd take a newspaper out in the yard, set it afire and singe that chicken. Then she'd wash it off, cut it up and fry it. My, we really enjoyed that. Of course she'd use pork lard to fry in. She'd get the chicken frying and she'd make white gravy in that grease where the chicken had fried. That made the best white gravy we ever eat. We'd pour that gravy over our biscuits and, my, we had such good eatin'.

After dad would sell his cotton in the fall of the year, he'd go to A. Allen's Store in Gainesville and buy our winter clothes. You see, we just got two pair of overalls a year and one pair of work shoes. The overalls were thick when you got them in the winter. You'd wear one pair all week and they'd be plenty dirty with this Georgia red clay. My sisters would have to wash our overalls with lye soap. They had a big black pot and they'd put the overalls in the pot and boil them. They had what they called a battling stick and a battling bench. After they boiled the overalls, they'd get them out of the pot and put them on the battling bench. It was us boys job to take that battling stick and beat those clothes, beat the dirt out of them. Each pair of those overalls would get washed every other week through the winter. By the time summer came they were getting sort of thin. Having them thick during the winter made them comfortable to wear.

Those days passed away and we come to the place where we could find a job somewhere and make a little money to go to the store to buy things to eat. In the early days of White County, a lot of stores didn't have any meat for sale because they didn't have any way of keeping the meat. There was just dry goods and hardware and canned food. When I was about 14 years old I was working for a neighbor and made about a dollar a day. That was big money. I'd go down to the store and buy a can of tomatoes – I think they cost a dime – and they had these boxes of sodie crackers. I'd buy those sodie crackers, take them home, cut those tomatoes up, pour them in a bowl, and put a little salt and black pepper on them, and crumble up those crackers. That was some good eatin'.

After times got better and there were restaurants in the community, we thought it was just real wonderful to go to a restaurant and get a meal, maybe for 50 cents. In Cleveland there was a restaurant where the new courthouse is standing. You would go there and buy your dinner. I don't think they ever thought about cooking a breakfast there. It was very seldom we got to go to a restaurant for a meal. We're living in such a different day now where there's so many restaurants. Very few do home cooking because they can eat out about as cheap as they can grow their vegetables and fix and cook them.

Later on, when I became 15, dad rented the adjoining farm from a Mrs. Carter. Her husband, John Carter, had passed away and she moved to Texas with some of her family that was out there. The farm had a good house on it and about 100 acres of land dad rented. For $100 a year we would sub-rent the place to somebody to live in the house and help farm the land. We grew corn to feed the stock and the hogs. One job I always dreaded was pulling fodder that grows on the corn, but we had to have fodder for the mules to eat. I remember getting stung by packsaddle, a big worm about the size of your little finger that had stickers on its back. They really hurt when they stung. Dad chewed tobacco and he'd take a piece of tobacco out of his mouth, put it on the sting, and that would sort of ease the pain. The packsaddle loved to eat that fodder. We wouldn't see them when we came to the corn stalk, stripping the blades off. Those were hard days.

Each March us boys would always look forward to seeing the mountains burn off. It was always a real pretty sight for us to see the big line of fire across these high mountains around here. The first fire we'd usually see was Skitts Mountain. Later, I would become very acquainted with Skitts Mountain because I would go fox hunting there. The farmers in the community would set the mountains on fire and we loved to sit out at night and see those rings of fire going up. The fires wouldn't burn out of control like they do now because they were burned every year. All that was left to burn was the leaves that had fallen off that year, so there was no tree damage when they burned off the mountains.

This is just my opinion, but when the government stopped the burning off of these mountains we lost those huge chestnut trees. The leaves got to piling up from year to year on top of one another and that created a fungus that killed the chestnut trees. By 19 and 30 all those chestnut trees were dead. They'd use chestnut trees to cut rails out of to make fences to hold the cattle in. That chestnut was lasting wood; it would make a fence that would last for maybe 20 years.

Another thing about burning off those mountains: in the spring of the year the grass could come up. In May, farmers like my dad would round up their dry cattle and brand them. We would keep the milking cows at home but the dry cattle would be rounded up by a couple of fellas on horses and my dad in a wagon. They'd turn those cattle in the road and drive them. They didn't have to worry about meeting traffic then; there was scarcely any traffic in the roads. They'd drive them all the way from here to Helen which was about 15 miles. They'd go through Helen to the foot of the mountains, to the home of a man who was accustomed to doing this when farmers would bring their cattle. They didn't have any fence there, but the man would take the cattle back up in the mountains to let them feed off the grass. My father would pay him something to keep salt out for the cattle. There was plenty of water coming out of those branches in the mountains for the cattle to drink. Settlers had killed out all the bears and the coyotes that could harm the cattle. The man would just check in on the cattle occasionally to see they were all right. Then in the fall of the year, about the middle of October, dad would get his men on horses again and they would go to the man's house. Then they would all go up in the mountains, round up the cattle, and they'd drive them back home.

When I was 15 years old my dad had his house covered with pine shingles. They wouldn't last but about ten years before you needed to reshingle the house. He got a man to bring his shingle mill and that was before the days when they was pulled by a gasoline engine. Most all of the shingle mills then was pulled by a steam engine.

Those steam engines had a big, long boiler. They were about 15 foot long from the firebox to the end where the smoke-stack went up. The body leading off that firebox had pipes in it, long pipes that you pumped full of water. Then you built a fire in the firebox and that smokestack would draw the fire. They called it a flume.

Water in those pipes created the steam so you always had to set those steam engines down next to a stream. My dad had a branch in his pasture so they set the shingle mill down by the bank of that branch. They built a dam and dammed up that branch to where it would be two to three feet deep. They'd run a pipe from the boiler of the engine into that branch and it would pump water into the engine. You had a gauge that set on top of the boiler that would tell you how much steam you had. With a shingle mill you needed at least 60 pounds. A sawmill you'd needed 100 pounds. You fired that engine and cut pine blocks into four-inch strips, that was the width of a shingle. They were 18 inches long. Each steam engine had a whistle, like a train, set on top of it. They had a chain hooked to a lever on the whistle. When you pulled that chain, that whistle would blow. At 12 o'clock every day, when a sawmill or a shingle mill was in the community, the fireman would pull that whistle. They'd shut down and eat dinner, take off for an hour. We in the fields, we'd hear that whistle and we'd know it was time to go to dinner.

My neighbor's boy, he was a little mischievous, and his dad had several cattle. He picked out a steer and learned that steer to ride like a horse. He had a bridle on it and he rode that steer, just showing out, over to the shingle mill one day. He made the mistake of riding the steer, just to show how he could make it mind, between a pond and the engine. The fireman, being kind of mean, when my neighbor got to the deepest place next to the pond, that fireman blew the whistle. The steer left the ground, and the boy landed in the middle of the pond.

Those were hard days, but they were days when neighbors would be neighbors to one another. When one of the farmers would get behind with his crops, a bunch of his neighbors would gather in and help the man, no charge. But those days is long been past. You can have next-door neighbors now and not even know their names, never associate with them, which is really bad. One of Jesus' commandments was to love thy neighbor as thyself. If we don't know who our neighbor is, it's a little difficult to love them. But when we associate with them and help one another, that's proof of love.

In the 13th chapter of St. John, starting with the 34th verse, it says, "A new commandment I give unto you, that ye love one another; as I have loved you, that ye also love one another. By this shall all men know that ye are my disciples, if ye have love one to another."

Love is not love until it is given away. To illustrate what I'm talking about, I could have one hundred dollars in my pocket and tell one of my neighbors that I've got one hundred dollars here for you. But as long as it stays in my pocket, it would not help my neighbor one bit. The only benefit he's going to get out of it is when I give it to him; then he can get some good out of it. That's what Jesus meant when he said you have to give your love before you can tell anybody, "I love you."

3

CONVERSION AND A CALLING

In September of 19 and 31, the night before my conversion, quite simply I'm ashamed to speak of it, but I had begun drinking. And I was using tobacco in all three forms – smoking, chewing and dipping snuff.

I was attending a revival at Macedonia Methodist Church, but the crowd was so large you could hardly get a seat. A bunch of us boys were standing on the outside and I proposed to two of my friends – which turned out in later years to be my brothers-in-law – that we go get us something to drink. A man lived up the road near Leaf Post Office that sold whiskey. We walked up there and we asked him what he had.

"I've got wine and got some moonshine," he said.

I suggested, "Well mix us up a pint of wine and whiskey."

That was the wrong thing to do. That's a bad combination. But he mixed us a pint and we didn't drink it up there, for some reason we thought we would wait until we got back to the church. When we walked back to the revival, the service was over and people were all outside. At that time they had the old oil lamps on the side of the church and they had blowed all of them out. We were trying to decide what we were going to do with our pint of whiskey because there were so many people outside the church we couldn't drink it.

"The church is dark and there's nobody inside," I said. "Let's go in there and divide it."

So we went inside the church and drank our whiskey and wine, just us three. That was some mean stuff. By the time I got home that night, I couldn't walk without holding on to something.

I laid down and had mind enough to think, "Well, now you don't want to die like this."

So I murmured the "Lord's Prayer" as I went off to sleep. That night I had a terrible dream. I had me a pint of whiskey and we had a neighbor that loved his drink. In my dream I decided I would walk down to my neighbor's house and offer him a drink. I went up and knocked on his door and asked him to go out to the barn with me. When we got out there I told him I had something to drink and asked if he wanted some.

He said, "Oh yeah."

I handed him the pint and he turned that thing up and drank about half of it. I was disappointed and didn't like that, so I just stuck the whiskey back in my pocket and told him I would be going home. I walked down his driveway, got in the road, and started back home. Then I heard what I thought at first was a fox horn for fox hunting. I stopped to listen, and it got louder and louder.

I thought, "That's not a fox horn; that must be a trumpet."

I remember in my dream looking back towards Yonah Mountain, and fire was rolling to the sky.

"Oh, my, this must be the end of time," I thought.

I could see objects going up in front of the fire, and I figured they were being saved. I started jumping as high as I could, trying to go up, and I woke myself up trying to jump. But believe it or not I could still hear that trumpet in the walls of my dad's old house. I went back to sleep. The next night at the revival, when they gave the altar call, I was one of the first to go up, asking God's forgiveness. The last drink I ever had was that pint of whiskey and wine in Macedonia Methodist Church.

So the next week they started a revival over at Union Grove Holiness Church. I didn't know that there was any difference in doctrines in churches at that time, so I just went to every revival. At Union Grove, they preached the baptism of the Holy Ghost with the evidence of speaking in tongues. I went down to the altar and received my baptism with the evidence of speaking in tongues. I started attending the Holiness Church because they had services more frequent than the Methodists and the Baptists, especially through the wintertime.

In the fall of 19 and 32, the Lord had begun to deal with me about preaching. Every two weeks on a Saturday I'd walk three miles over to Rob Pilgrim's. Rob was a barber.

One day I said to Rob, "The Lord's been dealing with me about preaching."

Rob walked around in front of me - he had a curious way of looking at you. He looked me straight in the eye and said, "Asa, you never could testify, much less preach."

That was not too encouraging.

Then it came a snow in December of 19 and 32, about eight inches deep. The Lord just kept dealing with me and I couldn't sleep. So I got up about 12 o'clock at night and dressed as warmly as I could, and went down to dad's pasture. I had a place in my mind that I wanted to go to where a spring comes out of the side of the hill and makes a little branch. I went and knelt down there and began to pray. I guess I prayed for 30 minutes and realized my feet was getting cold. My dad and mother had built their first home over in the field with a log barn and four stables.

That old barn was still standing and it came in my mind, "Why don't you go over to the old barn and pray?"

I made my way across the field to the old barn and I prayed until about four o'clock in the morning. I decided it was time to go back. I didn't think I woke anybody up when I left my dad's house. I didn't want them to know I had been out praying. So I went back, undressed, and got back in the bed and slept a little while.

After Christmas of 19 and 32, there was a young man by the name of Buford Palmer that had been called to preach. He was a musician and a composer of songs and also a preacher. He was a rare fella, very quick to act without much consideration. He come by the house, the day after Christmas, and said, "Asa, I started on my evangelistic tour. I want you to go with me and be my singer."

I had gone to some singing schools run by A.W. Wofford, and learned about the chromatic scale and shaped notes. I could follow those notes and do a little singing.

I said, "Yeah, I'll go with you."

We got mother to fix us some dinner, and after we ate we set out for Habersham Mills walking. I guess it took us three or four hours, and on the journey I confided in Buford about the Lord dealing with me about preaching. He didn't give me no encouragement, but we went on that Friday night to a home there in Habersham Mills. I led the singing then turned the service over to Buford. We had a service Saturday night – same thing. I did the singing with the congregation helping me, then turned the service over to Buford. Buford announced after the close of the services Saturday night that we'd be having a meeting up at D. Wheeler's, just outside of Clarkesville, on Sunday at 2:30 p.m.

We spent the night at Brother Pinky Robertson's at Habersham Mills. The next morning they fixed us a good breakfast. We walked to Clarkesville on Sunday which was New Year's Day, 19 and 33.

We got up there and there was a crowd of young people up there, mostly girls. I did the singing and turned the service over to Buford.

Buford got up and said, "Well, folks, we got a new preacher today."

I looked around to see who had come in. Nobody had come in.

He said, "Brother Dorsey is going to preach."

It was like a thunderbolt. All I knowed to do was to go to prayer. I went down on my knees and began praying.

The Spirit spoke to me and said, "Now you'll make your decision. Whatever you decide now will be final."

So I decided I would try it. I got up and borrowed the preacher's Bible and read five verses of the eighth chapter of Romans which began with: "There is therefore now no condemnation to them which are in Christ Jesus, who walk not after the flesh, but after the Spirit."

I went to talking about what I read; I talked for what might have been fifteen minutes. I felt like we ought to give the people the chance to seek God, so I told them to vacate the chairs on the front row, and turn them around towards where I was standing. We would make that the altar.

The young people filled that altar up. There were eight people saved that evening. That set me afire.

When we were walking home on Monday morning Buford said, "Well, Brother Dorsey, I think God just took my gift and gave it to you."

So I come home seeking a place to preach, and went to preaching in homes, most times on Friday nights at whatever home would open the door.

And I learned later that A.W. Wofford knew that God was going to call me to preach before it happened.

I attended a singing school down at White Creek Baptist Church in 19 and 31 and 32. A.W. Wofford was teaching the singing school and he taught during the day from eight o'clock in the morning to noon. He gave us an hour for dinner. He took back in at one and taught 'til four. This went on for two weeks. On the last Friday of the second week he invited all the parents in to hear their children lead a song. We were using Stamp-Baxter's new book. I must confess my main reason for going to singing school was to be with the young folks. But I did learn a little which was on the chromatic scale, length, pitch, power and quality. And I learned the notes: do, rae, me fa, so, la, te, do. That made me able to sing a little on a familiar song.

On the last Friday of the last week, when the families had gathered in to hear their children sing, he had each student to get up and lead a song. I set there dreading my time because I couldn't lead a song.

He was a stern old teacher and he looked at me when my time come and said, "All right Asa, it's your time."

I just reached and got a book and thought, "Well, I can sing one as good as I can another."

So I just opened the hymnbook, and fortunately it come open at a little three-quarter page song on the left, uncomplicated, just a straight, simple song. I called out my song number and the organist – we had an old-time pump organ at that time – she turned to the number. Then I had to announce the title of the song. The title was, "My Friend Get Right With God."

I remember so well when I announced the title, Mr. Wofford stood to his feet, and asked, "Asa, can I help you lead that song?"

That saved my day. We really sang that song. I always wondered, "Why was I the only one he volunteered to help lead their song?"

Jesse Savage was a Baptist minister down at Skitts Mountain

Baptist Church. His mother, Mrs. Ernie Savage, passed away on December 30, 19 and 77. I was asked to have a part in the funeral, so I went to the home about an hour before we was to go to the church. In those days, country people, more often than not, brought the bodies back to their homes. I was standing out in the yard talking with a group of men. Mr. Wofford come up and I was surprised to see him, because he was on a walking stick and getting sort of feeble.

He come straight to me and shook hands with me and he asked, "Brother Dorsey, do you remember attending my singing school at White Creek?"

I said, "Yes, Brother Wofford, I've thought of that all my life."

He said, "Well, I've been planning to tell you this for years. Do you remember on the last Friday of the singing school when each student led a song?"

I answered, "Yes, I remember that very well."

He said, "Do you remember me getting up and volunteering to help you lead that song?"

I answered, "Yes, Mr. Wofford, I have always wondered why you did that?"

"Well, that's what I wanted to tell you," he explained. "When you announced the title of that song, God spoke to me and said, 'this is one of my ministers.' And I wanted to have a part in your ministry."

That was two years before I ever started thinking about preaching.

4

A HOME WITH HOLINESS

When I started preaching – me being limited in an education because I just went to the fourth grade in school – I didn't know anything about church doctrine. I thought a church was a church. I found out, after I went to preaching, that they had different doctrines, and some felt animosity against one another because of the difference in doctrines. I wasn't preaching nobody's doctrine; I was just preaching what I read in the Bible. It turned out in the cottage meetings, the Holiness people was the only ones that would come to listen to me.

In the fall of 19 and 33, I met Buford Skelton. Buford worked at the First National Bank in Gainesville. He had visited Union Grove Holiness Church, where he got saved and was called to preach.

Buford came to the fodder field where I was pulling fodder and said, "I feel like you and me need to have a tent meeting."

I said, "That suits me."

We went over to see Wiley Warwick because he had a tent. There was a lady visiting the Warwick's that had a new car that she said she would loan us, a 1933 Studebaker. We borrowed it and drove to Cleveland. Buford said he felt like we ought to go up towards the Asbestos Community. When we got to Asbestos we stopped at Will Blalock's. He lived in an old store-house, there in the back rooms. We told Will we were looking for a place to put up the tent, and we were going over to a nearby knoll to pray a while.

After prayer, we come back to the car and drove across the creek to the next house which was Ollie Turner's. We saw Ollie sitting out on the steps, and told him we were looking for a place to put up a gospel tent.

Ollie said, "Well, we got that big grove out there, if you want to put it out there anywhere, go ahead."

That's what we were looking for.

We come back the next day and put the tent up. It was the last of September. It got pretty chilly at night, but we ran for two weeks and had 51 converts. One night L.G. Howard's mother went into a trance around the altar. John, her husband, got uneasy about her. She looked like a dead person lying there. He would come to Buford, then me, and say, "Is she all right?"

We assured him she was. About one o'clock that night we picked her up, put her in a wagon and hauled her home. She came to sometime before daylight and had a wonderful testimony to tell about her journey in the trance. L.G. was just seven when that happened. Trances used to be common back then.

When we stretched that tent in Ollie Turner's yard, the tent was about 40 feet in diameter and we would close it during the day. Living near Ollie were some boys that would play with his sons. There was Bill and Jack Turner, and Felton Hefner and another Hefner brother – I can't recall his name. But they'd all get together and play. Ollie Turner had a big old billy goat, and them boys had aggravated that goat until he'd gotten so ornery they couldn't do nothing with him. Those boys would come to the tent service every night and saw men who were formerly drunkards come to the altar and get saved, and what a change it made in their lives.

So one day they was having a time with that billy goat and one of them said, "I think what he needs is a case of old-time religion."

They made a halter out of rope with a long lead on it. They led the goat down to the tent during the day when no one was around and got him in front of the altar. The altar was a 1 X 10 just nailed to some posts that come up from the ground. All of them boys combined couldn't make that old goat kneel. They tell me a billy goat will die before they'll kneel.

One of the boys had the bright idea, "I know how we can get him down! Let's run the rope under that altar and we'll pull him down."

They started pulling on the goat, and he tore that altar completely up. We went in that night for the service and we couldn't imagine what had happened to that altar. A day or two later, one of the boys told us they tried to get the billy goat to get religion but he wouldn't cooperate.

Another story about the tent meeting there that's rather comical had to do with a fella that lived up above the tent. He wasn't in favor of the tent being there. Buford Skelton and myself were staying in the Vass Hefner home. There was some big woods above the Hefner house and Buford and myself would go up in the woods to pray. The road come down by the Hefner house and on out around by Ollie Turner's home. The man that had some dislike about the tent being there, he come walking down the road one morning and heard us up in the woods praying. We'd get happy and shout along.

He went down the road and stopped at a neighbor's house and said, "Well, I found out why those Holiness people shout so much – they get out in the woods and practice all day."

I was asked to help preach in a Baptist revival, and that sounded good to me. I went the first Sunday night, and I got up and read the scripture I thought would fit from the 62nd chapter of Isaiah, the 10th verse: "Go through, go through the gates; prepare ye the way of the people; cast up, cast up the highway; gather out the stones, lift up a standard for the people."

My subject was lifting up a standard for the people. I just preached what I'd read in the Bible, and noticed when I got through and sat down, the Baptist preacher got up and tried to fix what I'd preached. And a lady come to me after the service and said, "Preacher, if what you preached was in the Bible, I ain't never read it."

Well, I knew I had read it; that's the reason I used it. So I seen they didn't want me, and I didn't go back.

So I started attending Union Grove. I joined the church and was baptized the first Sunday in October of 19 and 33, a frosty chilly morning, down in Brother Jesse Lovell's fish-pond.

Union Grove was a Congregational Holiness Church founded in 1922. Let me tell you a little about the history of the Congregational Holiness Church. A man named Watson Sorrow was a rough character that was a clown in a Vaudeville show and liked to drink a lot. He told me he would come to cities like Atlanta and get high on whiskey. Then he'd go down the street and every black man he'd meet, he'd kick him off the street. And he was also a big gambler.

But in 19 and 10, an evangelist by the name of B.F. Duncan went to Abbeville, S.C. and started a revival. Watson Sorrow and some of his buddies had been down to the big spring there in Abbeville to do some gambling. He had started back home and went by a church and heard a man talking. Brother Sorrow decided he would go in and see who it was. The man talking was B.F. Duncan and he was a very persuasive Holiness Preacher. When Preacher Duncan gave an altar call, Watson Sorrow went to the altar and was saved. Later he became a Holiness preacher. At that time Duncan belonged to the Pentecostal Holiness Church. The Pentecostal Holiness is an offshoot of what happened in California in the early 1900s when a black man began to fast and pray and received the baptism of the Holy Spirit with evidence of speaking in tongues. He began a revival at a place called Azusa Street in Los Angeles that spread like wildfire. So many Holiness Churches sprang from that. The Pentecostal Holiness Church and the Fire Baptized Holiness Church was formed out of that revival that started in California.

J.H. King came to Royston, Georgia, and built a college which is Emmanuel College. King was head of that college and Watson Sorrow was a preacher there. King taught if a man lived in God's highest will he'd never be sick. He didn't believe in taking any kind of medicine, not even an aspirin, but Watson Sorrow differed from him.

Brother Sorrow said he believed that divine healing was in the atonement, but he did not feel the Bible condemned medical science, since Luke, a physician, was one of the writers of the four Gospels. So the feeling between J.H. King and Watson Sorrow was not too good.

In about 19 and 19 the Pentecostal Holiness Church had established an orphanage in Falcon, North Carolina. They had a little girl to come down with appendicitis, and since they were under Brother King's supervision, they couldn't take her to the doctor. They just gathered together and had prayer. And someone said he got an answer to the prayer from God and that God had healed the little girl.

A testimony was written and published in the *Advocate*, which is the official Pentecostal newspaper, saying that God had healed the little girl. But by the time this testimony got to Franklin Springs near Royston and the paper was printed, the little girl was dead and had been buried for several days. When that came out in the *Advocate*, Watson Sorrow contacted them and said the paper had printed a lie, that God did not heal the girl. So J.H. King didn't say anything to Watson Sorrow, he just called his committee together and excommunicated Brother Sorrow.

So when they turned Brother Sorrow out in about 19 and 20, other ministers turned in their resignation. That left a group of ministers without a church. They met in January of 19 and 21 at Bethel Church, just this side of Royston, and organized the Congregational Holiness Church because they wanted it to be governed not by a board, but governed by the members.

Watson Sorrow, his dad was an old-time Methodist preacher and that's where he got a lot of his Holiness roots. Those roots go back to John Wesley and his experience of sanctification, Wesley felt like God poured a bucket of "liquid love" on him. Wesley taught sanctification as a second definite work of Grace, and so did the Holiness.

The Union Grove Congregational Holiness Church was founded in 19 and 22 and B.F. Duncan was the organizer. That was the first church I pastored – Union Grove – while I was single and just 18 years old. I pastored there from November 1 of '33 to November 1 of '34, and then 10 other churches after that.

I also ran a lot of tent meetings. The last tent meeting I had was in Helen with Wiley and Icie Warwick. Sister Warwick would preach one night and me the next night. One night I remember well was with Brother Franklin. He was an old, original mountain man. He'd take spells of shouting and close his eyes – you had to get out of his way or get run over. So at a service one night in Helen in 19 and 35, right next to the Chattahoochee River, where the Holiness Church is now, we was all standing up on the rostrum around the old organ singing. Silva Westmoreland was the organist. Brother

Franklin couldn't carry a tune in a bucket. He got happy and started shoutin', and he went to dancin'. We had a 2' by 8' board just
nailed up on studs there for the people that sat in the choir, and we
had curtains around the choir. Brother Franklin backed into the
choir's bench – it hit him right in the calf of the leg – and zoop! –
he went out from under that curtain.

A lady jumped up in the tent and shouted, "Lord, have mercy,
he's gone in the river."

In a few minutes, Brother Franklin came creeping back around,
got him a seat, and sat down.

I had no formal training, just what I read in the Bible. I knew if
I was going to preach I had to know the Bible. I graduated from
school in the fourth grade, but I had a mother that was a graduate
of the Blue Back Speller. She would spell to us children. I remember one word she spelt was, "incomprehensibility," and another
was, "acidificity," and other such words as that. When I started
preaching and reading the Bible, there were words I couldn't pronounce, so mother would cut them up in syllables. She learned me
how to do that, and pronounce them, and tell me their meaning.
That's the education I got, from my mother, reading the Bible.

I learned right off the Bible is a set of principles, but we have
to work out the details. Just like a house plan where the carpenter
has to work out the details.

I remember the night I was ordained, there was 19 of us young
preachers ordained that night. Preacher Duncan was there; he was
the man that come through here preaching Holiness and organized
Union Grove. They had us to stand up at the altar, and the other
preachers there come around and congratulated us.

Preacher Duncan took me by the hand, hugged my neck, and
he said, "Now, Asa, get you a band and put it around your head."

I thought, "Now what does he mean, get you a band and put it
around your head?"

He knew how young preachers would take the "big head" some time, and felt like they knew a lot more than what they did.

I always appreciated preachers that had a good sense of humor, like Brother Watson Sorrow. Brother Sorrow was telling me how he was in South Georgia at a meeting and this lady come up to him and said, "I want you to pray for my husband; he is just so wicked."

Brother Sorrow was trying to use scripture to give her advice to return evil with good. In Romans the 12th chapter, starting with the 19th verse, it reads: "Dearly beloved, avenge not yourselves, but rather give place unto wrath: for it is written, vengeance is mine, I will repay, saith the Lord. Therefore if thine enemy hunger, feed him, if he thirst, give him drink; for in so doing thou shalt heap coals of fire on his head."

Bother Sorrow said, "Well have you tried heaping coals of fire on his head?"

She answered, "No, but I've tried scalding water."

When Holiness first come to these mountains it was not much liked by the other religions. There was a lot of suspicion about speaking in tongues and some folks thought tongues come from Satan. One night while I was preaching I felt a jarring of the altar. Somebody had thrown a rock and it come through the tent and hit the rostrum. Then here come another one, but I just kept preaching. The tent was sort of down below the road, and I think they was standing up in the road throwing rocks. We didn't try to find out who is was; we expected opposition back then.

I had a meeting at Blue Creek, not far from Blue Creek Church. A fella lived in a home there and wanted me to bring my tent and have a meeting. This was in about 19 and 35 and I was still single then. I carried my tent up there and put it up. Course there was a lot of opposition. I found out later there was men that walked the road with axe handles and did different things to inflict harm on people. I just kept preaching.

One day I got a letter from my uncle, A.L. Dorsey, who was an ordinary in White County.

He said in the letter, "Asa, I'd just like to call this to your attention. I understand you're in a tent meeting on Blue Creek and I understand you're having a lot of opposition."

I reckon the opposing people had went to him and talked to him.

His letter said, "My thinking is the best way to accomplish good is to weaken opposition. If you'd just take your tent down and move out, that would weaken opposition."

But I didn't pay it no mind.

Years later a man that attended Blue Creek Baptist Church all of his life come to me and said, "Asa, I've been planning to tell you and never could find an opportunity. I got saved in your tent meeting at Blue Creek."

At a meeting in Cleveland in 19 and 45, a young man tried to set the tent afire. Some men under the tent jumped up and put it out. I was preaching, and the son of a family opposed to Holiness lit a newspaper and threw it up on the tent. I just kept preaching. Some others saw him do it and he was prosecuted for it by the law. They called me to testify. When I got on the stand, I told them that I understood his opposition. I said I just chose to pray for him, and would appreciate the court showing him some mercy. He got a pretty light sentence. We always tried to respond to opposition with love.

I was preaching one night at a tent meeting in Kennesaw, Georgia. This man that weighed about 270 pounds and was about six-foot-three inches tall got up from his seat and started down the aisle toward me.

It was just the mercy of the Lord, I thought, "Well, he's coming to the altar."

So I jumped across the altar and went to meet him. I stuck out my hand to get him by his hand, and he stuck his hand out.

He asked me, "Preacher, did I understand you to say it was wrong to use tobacco?"

I answered, "Well, if I didn't, I meant to."

By that time some of the supporters that supported the tent meeting had formed a ring around me and started praying. The man saw he was surrounded and he tried to pull loose. But I was about 20 years old then and had quite a bit of strength. I weighed about 180 pounds. I grabbed his hand with both of mine and I was holding on pretty good. But finally he broke loose and tore through the crowd and got out of there.

They told me the next day, "He's run every preacher out of Kennesaw that's come here preaching Holiness!"

But you know, that man come back to the tent meeting every night and never did give any more trouble.

5

MARRIAGE, WORK AND GAINING COMPASSION

In 19 and 35, I was pretty well wore out from tent meetings, so I decided to visit my brother, B.C., that was living in Detroit, Michigan. B.C. was named after the first funeral director of Hall County, Albert Barton Cecil Dorsey. B.C. worked at General Springs and Bumper Company and was acquainted with the employment agent and the superintendent of that factory. The factory got contracts from Dodge and Ford. Dodge included Plymouth, Dodge and all the Chrysler line. They also had a contract for a car that was manufactured then called the Terraiplane. Hudson made the Terraiplane. Then they also made a car just called the Hudson.

This factory made the bumpers for all these cars; that's all they did there. They had a nickel department and a buffing department. They had to form the bumpers first out of steel using a blueprint. Then they were polished and went over to the nickel tanks. They had bars of nickel on each side of those tanks, and they'd lower a bunch of bumpers down in the tanks on a rack, and some how or other that nickel would leave the bar and go onto those bumpers. Then the bumpers were buffed. After buffing, they were sent to the chromium tank, and then buffed again.

B.C. asked me, "Why don't you stay awhile and get a job since you're up here?"

Well, I thought that might be a good idea, but there was employment lines everywhere you went. This was in the Depression.

B.C. said, "I'll write you a little note. When you get to the employment agent, give him the note."

You see the employment agent would come out the door of his office, stand on the steps and the line of men would just file by. I was in the long line. I guess there was at least 100 men in that line, and the employment agent would just motion everybody by. He come to me and started to motion me by, and I held out the note from B.C. to him. He read the note, stepped back, and told me to come in his office.

I went in his office and he said, "When do you want to start to work?"

I answered, "Well any time."

He said, "Be here at 11 o'clock tonight and start on the midnight shift."

That was the middle of October of 35, and I worked there until June of 36.

When I went up to Detroit I was going with Annie Kate Palmer, the girl that later become my wife. Her oldest brother and another boy from the White Creek District of White County both got jobs through the influence of B.C. Annie Kate was the daughter of Edward Palmer and Dovie Bell Davidson, and they lived here in Mossy Creek.

Annie and I went to the same school at Woodlawn. But then I left school and she continued on. In 19 and 31 I went to Mossy Creek Campground. I hadn't been around Annie in a good little bit. She was 13 years old and I thought she had become the most attractive young lady I'd ever seen. There was a large spring there at Mossy Creek and the young folks would make it a habit of walking to the spring, just to be together and get a drink of water. I asked Annie if she'd go to the spring with me and she consented. We started dating and dated for about a year. Then we parted ways – she went her way and I went mine. Soon after that I was called to preach.

I want to say how thankful I am that the Lord directed me to marry Annie Kate, because I almost made an error in that decision. Confused, I went before the Lord in prayer and asked him to please direct me. He knew who would be best for me and showed me in a vision that it would be Annie Kate Palmer. I didn't have a car back then so I just saddled up dad's old mule and rode down to Annie's house the next night. She was in high school then and living on the Ray Palmer Road. I knocked on the door and she come to the door and invited me in. We began to date regular until I went to Detroit to work.

In April of '36 the Gainesville tornado hit and Annie was in the middle of that. She was living in a brick building with the Kenimer sisters next to a hosiery plant in Gainesville. She said it turned so dark and when she looked out of the window of the brick house she could see the air all full of stuff. She was trying to find a safe place to hide. She finally just went into the dining room and just balled up in the corner of the room. When the storm hit it took the top off the house She said it drove a 2' x 4' that was split through the brick wall, and it just missed her. Of course they were all soaking wet. She was afraid of storms all during her life after that tornado.

I decided I'd worked long enough in Detroit, so I caught a bus and come back to White County in June of '36. Annie Kate and I decided to get married on July the ninth of 19 and 36, when she was 18 and I was 20.We were married in the home of Robert

Pilgrim because up until that time there had been no marriage ceremonies in the Union Grove Holiness Church. Some of the older members didn't believe in men and women even sitting together in church. One of the deacons in the church said, "I'll bc die, the church is no sparking grounds." So we were married in the home of Robert and Mary John Pilgrim.

I believe stronger than ever that Annie was a God-given mate. With nine children, 22 grandchildren, and at the time of her death, 18 great-grandchildren, I never heard her one time lift her voice while correcting any of them. She was such a wonderful example to me. I didn't understand for years why Annie never complimented my ministry when I preached, so I never knew what she liked or didn't like. I come to appreciate that in later years because it gave me the liberty to talk about whatever the Lord would have me to talk about. She was a precious, faithful companion for 61 years and in that time we never had a fuss. We had some disagreements, but we would sit down and talk about those disagreements, and if we couldn't settle them in our conversation, we'd join hands, get on our knees and pray a while about it. Some way or other we'd get up from prayer and the disagreement would be gone.

I can't imagine my life without her. She was a better woman than I was a man. She was more humble. The Dorseys have a fiery streak and it's a little hard to manage that sometimes. She was always calm and collected. My ministry was much stronger because of her. She gave me a lot of inspiration. She would go with me to visit people in hospitals and that was a big help. She was running over with a quiet, unselfish goodness. I didn't have that; it was something I had to copy. She died here at home on November the third, 19 and 97, following a battle with cancer.

But after we were married, we went back up to Detroit and I worked there all winter. The next spring in April, we come back to

Georgia and rented a house down on Mossy Creek for three dollars a month, which we thought was pretty high rent at that time. We didn't have any furniture to go in the house. We had an aunt named Annie Thrasher; she was an Alexander before she married Dr. Bart Thrasher. They'd spend the winters in Florida and the summers here in Georgia. He died when I was just a small boy. But he must have left my aunt an annuity because she drew a pension, as best I can remember about fifty dollars every month. That was a lot of money in those days. My aunt was a very religious lady and she supported my ministry.

Since the spring had come my aunt had come back from Florida and she wanted to live with Annie and myself. We didn't have any furniture so she took us to Gainesville to the B.H. Moore Furniture store. She bought us a cook stove, a range that had a warming oven. We'd never been used to anything like that. She also bought us a corner cabinet and a pie safe, four chairs, a table, two iron bedsteads and two sets of folding springs. In those days there was no such thing for us as buying a mattress, you had to make your own mattress. The ladies would sew sheeting together and leave the top of it open, and we'd stuff that with wheat straw. We'd put that on the springs and it made what we thought was a very comfortable bed. All of that she purchased cost eighty-five dollars. She just gave it to us as a gift and we really appreciated that.

In '38 I built us a house in White Creek where my daughter Trilla Pruitt now lives. We lived there 29 years. All our children grew up there. After I got the house built, a neighbor come to see me; he was one of the deacons at Union Grove. He wanted to see if I would preach again at Union Grove. So I was elected to preach there in '38 and stayed there 'til '43. Of course, back then, a pastor didn't get paid a salary like they do now, so you had to work to help provide for your family.

After returning from Detroit in '37, I bought a shingle mill and started sawing shingles. I only had to hire one hand to help me. Then in 19 and 41, my brother, P.S., and myself purchased a sawmill and began to saw lumber. We sawmilled off and on until about 19 and 46. I remember in 19 and 41 when the Japanese bombed Pearl Harbor and we was at the sawmill, up on Blue Creek, the place we called Goat Neck. We was sawing up there and Bill Taylor come down from Cleveland and wanted to buy our outfit, so we had to go buy another one. Then we kept sawmilling until 19 and 46.

Back in 19 and 43 Barnett Blalock and Carlton Thurmond had started Cleveland Lumber Company. They'd bought a new planer, but the planer wouldn't work right, so Carlton decided to quit his part of it. Barnett come to the sawmill where I was and asked me if I'd take Carlton's place. I sold my part of the sawmill to C.M. Denton and I went up and become co-owner in what was then Cleveland Lumber Company. I advised Barnett the best thing we could do is join Southern Pine Inspection Bureau where we could begin to stamp our lumber. We got the planer running and put on their stamp, SPIB, which stood for Southern Pine Inspection Bureau. When the lumber had that stamp it sold a lot better. People knew we were abiding by the rules.

When we couldn't get the planer started I called Southern Pine Inspection Bureau and asked them for a millwright that worked on planing mills. I was told there was one in Athens, Georgia and they would send him right up. He come and started the planer up, seen what it was doing, and then shut it down. The straight edge lacked one hole. It was a new planer but the factory had failed to bore a hole for the straight edge. So he took the straight edge off and got a hole drilled and it went to working fine. So we started dressing a carload of lumber a day there.

This was during World War II and there was a ceiling price for the dressed lumber. We were paying as much for the lumber from the saw millers as the ceiling price was. But the company we was selling to told us they would make it up. The buyer would come in and leave us four one-hundred dollar bills and tell us to ship them a carload of lumber. We did that a time or two. I began to think about the way we was selling lumber was against the law. So I told my partner, he was a deacon in a church I was pastoring, that it would make the headlines of the *Atlanta Constitution* if a Holiness preacher and his deacon were arrested for the black marketing of lumber. I told him I was going to sell out and he decided to sell his interest too. I contacted a planer over in Cornelia that had a large lumberyard and he said he would buy our outfit from us. So he sent a man over the next day to check what we had on the yard, the amount of footage in lumber that we had stacked. But he didn't get through it in one day - he told us it would take part of the next day. Over that night my partner decided not to sell his part. He made arrangements with another man to buy me out, so I got out of the business of planing lumber.

In 19 and 49 we rented a store, which was the old Floyd Kenimer Store, and we went into the grocery business. In the last part of '49 we decided to just buy some land and build us a store. So we bought four acres of land across the road from the store we were renting and in 19 and 50 we built what later become Dorsey Brothers Store.

In the fall of '50, P.S. and me also decided to go into the chicken business. We first built us a feed mill. We purchased a hammer mill and a mixer. I managed to get the dealership for White County from Ralston Purina Company to furnish extra feed we couldn't make. We stayed in the chicken business a year or two. In 19 and 53, the bottom just fell out of the price of broilers. Sometimes we only received twelve cents a pound for chickens picked up at the farm. We was paying $5.50 a bag for our feed shipped over in carloads to Cornelia. I seen we was going broke. Me and my brother, P.S. – we were both taking a salary per week out of the business – so I told him the business would not support both of our salaries.

I said, "I'm going to make you an offer, give or take."

He answered, "No I won't do that. I'll make you an offer, take."

So I took over the business – store, feed mill, and chicken business. I finally had to tell my creditors that I was broke. We met with our creditors in Gainesville. Joe Telford, my counselor, accompanied me to the meeting. He advised me I would be thrown into bankruptcy if I wasn't careful what I said to my creditors. But I did not have to file bankruptcy. My creditors took me at my word and let me pay as I could. Mr. Telford couldn't believe my word was enough. I mortgaged my home and farm for all the money I could get from the Federal Land Bank and sold what office equipment I had. I just went back to the farm and had hens put in my chicken houses and contracted with a company in Gainesville that would give me so much a dozen for the eggs produced.

When I went broke in 19 and 54, I notified the church that I felt like I was somewhat of a reproach to the church. I told them I wouldn't be preaching any more until I sort of got back on my feet. It come fall, the fall of '54, and I was there at home wondering what I was to do. I'd shut the mill down because it didn't have nothing to operate on.

I thought, well, instead of feeling sorry for myself, I needed to get out, do some work, and get up some perspiration So I went out to the barn and got the old mattock and went out to the end of the garden and went to digging, just digging for dear life. I got up a sweat and a little bird lit on the tree limb in view of me and began singing his heart out. I never will forget, I looked up at him, he had his chest throwed out towards me, just singing at the top of his voice.

I leaned on my mattock and looked at him and said, "Oh yes, no wonder you can sing, for God said you didn't have to gather in the barn because he'd feed you, and when you died he'd go to your funeral."

It says in the tenth chapter of Matthew, starting with verse 29, "Are not two sparrows sold for a farthing? And one of them shall not fall on the ground without your Father. But the very hairs on your head are numbered. Fear ye not therefore, ye are of more value than many sparrows."

I never had understood that verse like I understood it just then.

I looked up and said, "Thank you, Lord."

I picked up the mattock, throwed it across my shoulder and went to the house, happy as a lark because of what the presence of the Lord had just taught me.

That experience of going broke helped shape my ministry. After I lost what I had, I felt different toward others, and toward my calling to preach. I felt a sense of compassion that I'd never felt before. Prosperity theology – that God will bless you with material wealth if you have faith – is contrary to the New Testament and the teachings of Christ. The greatest gift God gives us is his saving Grace, which is divine love, and that leads to great inner peace.

A doctrine that's popular now with a lot of preachers that concerns me is the doctrine of God's blessing as shown by material prosperity. This doctrine of God giving you riches – and I've heard preachers say that the blessings of God means there should be a Cadillac in every garage – is not backed up by the Bible. Jesus never had anything to ride on until he made his entrance into Jerusalem, and he borrowed a colt to do that.

In 19 and 55 a man of the community asked me about starting

the mill back up. We had a hammer mill and mixer where the farmers would bring in the corn, run it through the hammer mill, and we had concentrates that we would mix with it and make cow feed. So this man come to me and asked if he could open the mill back up.

He said, "I'll do the work and you just let me use the mill. At the end of the week we'll divide what profit we have."

I told him, "Fine."

He did a good job for several months, but then he got sick and had to go in the hospital. So he contacted Verner Pilgrim to see if he could take up where he left off. Verner come and did the same thing for almost a year. He'd come to my house late on Saturday evening and bring what money he collected and we'd divide it. In the later part of '56, I decided to take Fonda Milling Company back over, and let Verner run the mill for me. We started making more feed.

At that time W.B. Robinson was a poultry man in Cleveland. He put out breeder hens where they'd hatch these baby chicks that were sold as broilers. He employed me to make the feed for him for his hens. We got going right good.

Cliff Blalock, Sr. bought a large boundary of land up on what they call Pig Valley Road and put up a hog farm there. By that time we'd started making horse feed, cow feed, and hog feed. My sons – Bradley and Phillip – were at the University of Georgia. They had an agricultural department at the college that formulated feed. So I contacted them and told them I wanted the best hog feed they could formulate. They didn't charge me nothing for it. When Cliff Blalock started his hog farm we put our feed up against Purina's and our feed come out ahead after weighing the hogs fed on the two different feeds.

We always tried to help the farmers succeed. Farmers would come in to get feed mixed and they'd buy other products. There was a man in White County that had a good-sized farm and several cattle. He'd come in and I always thought he was an honest man, so when he didn't have any money to pay for his feed, Verner would just put his name at the head of the ticket and put down what he got, and never thought to have him sign it. Then Verner would file that ticket away. At the end of the month I'd gather up those tickets and the secretary we had would send out statements. I sent this man a statement; he'd been buying pretty heavy and not paying.

He come in one day and said, "Preacher, you got me charged for stuff I didn't buy."

I said, "Well, let me get your tickets. I don't know a thing about it. Verner is the one that wrote the tickets out and you're the one that picked up the feed. But I don't think Verner would make a ticket to you when you hadn't gotten the feed."

I told him, "You take these tickets and set down over there and look through them. Every ticket that you think you didn't get, lay it out and you only pay me for them you think you got."

He sat over there and went through those tickets two or three times. Finally he got up and come into the back office where I was.

He said, "Well, I guess I got them all." Then he wrote me a check for it.

That's the way we did all our customers there, and it paid off.

I ran the mill until 19 and 71 when my son Bradley went to work for me. Father-like, I was a little apprehensive about letting Bradley have the mill. I thought, "Now he can't manage this thing."

But finally I convinced myself to let him have it. When I sold him the mill my yearly gross income was about a quarter of a million dollars. The second year Bradley had the mill on his own he went over a million dollars. On some Saturdays he would have 400 customers in nine hours. He built a real success out of Fonda Milling Company.

In the summer of 19 and 72, the year after I'd sold the mill to Bradley, I just wasn't satisfied to be idle. So one day I picked up the phone and called the Commissioner of Agriculture, Tommy Irvin, and asked him if he had anything that a fella like me could do? He said he'd talk to his employment man, a man by the name of Mr. Kelly, and see if they had anything open.

They had an opening in the inspector division and Mr. Kelly wrote me that they were considering me to be an inspector. I was satisfied with that because I had several revivals lined up that were already scheduled.

The afternoon that I got the letter, Mr. Kelly called me and said, "Have you received my letter?"

I answered, "Yes, I received it this morning."

He said, "Commissioner Irvin says for you to be down here Friday morning."

I said, "Well, I'm not in that big a hurry, I've got these revivals lined up."

He insisted, "Commissioner Irvin said for you to be down here."

So I went down and come back as an employee in the state agriculture inspectors department. At that time we had three divisions in inspection; there was North and Middle Georgia and South Georgia. I was in the North Georgia Division and there was, as best I can remember, 31 of us inspectors then. We'd have meetings and we'd usually have dinner at those meetings. Commissioner Irvin would always call for quiet and then ask me to offer thanks for the food. I appreciate the confidence he had in me. I worked for him for a little over 10 years. I wound up being a special investigator and that meant if other inspectors had a problem, I was to go and do my best to solve that problem. I enjoyed that work.

They gave me a retirement party there at the agriculture building in Atlanta. When the Commissioner had made his statement, they said it was my time to say something.

I said, "I've enjoyed working for the Department of Agriculture, but the biggest thing I'm going to miss is getting paid to visit my friends."

You see, all those people I went out to inspect become my friends. Some of them would invite me to have dinner with them. I learned they would work better to make improvements if I treated them with respect.

As I sit here thinking back over my life of 87 years, it's been a wonderful experience, and surely I'm the richest man in the world, not in bank accounts, bonds and dollars and cents, but that's not where true riches lie. I'm an heir to the Kingdom of God with Jesus Christ. What greater riches could you obtain? It's a wonderful experience to just love God with all your soul, mind, body and strength and to serve him in the beauty of Holiness.

And I've had the treasure of a God-given mate and nine wonderful children, plus grandchildren and great-grandchildren. Our children include Byron Sharrell, borned in '37; Miriam Louise, borned in '38; Thandal Haze, borned in '40; Bradley Wayne, borned in '42; Phillip Asa, borned in '44; Trilla Ann, borned in '45; Leethal Derrick, borned in '49; Desma Fern, borned in '52; and Fonda Dianne, borned in '57. Leethal and Desma died; Leethal in '82, and Desma in '93.

Sharrell owns a grocery store in Oxford, Alabama, and is on the city council there. He helped establish a radio station that plays mostly Christian music, and he speaks on the radio. He married Sherrill Chambers.

Miriam is a graduate of the nursing school at Georgia Baptist

Hospital and has been a registered nurse for 33 years. She married Dan Vandiver.

Thandal attended Tampa University on a football scholarship then left school to join the U.S. Marines. He was president of Eagle Aviation for 20 years in Columbia, South Carolina, and owned an automobile dealership. He's now an investor in several businesses. He married Cupie Abe.

Bradley graduated in accounting from the University of Georgia and purchased Fonda Milling Company from me in 19 and 71. He operated it until March of '97 when it burned. He married Sandra Bachelder.

Phillip is retired. He graduated from the University of Georgia as a second lieutenant in the Air Force and served as a pilot in Vietnam. He became a commercial pilot and married Cheryl Peters, also a commercial pilot.

Trilla graduated from North Georgia College and got her master's degree in counseling from West Georgia College. She's a counselor at White County High School. She married L.C. Pruitt.

Leethal graduated from high school and married his school sweetheart, Cheryl Gibbs. They had four children before he died in 19 and 82.

Desma graduated from high school and attended North Georgia Technical School. She had three children from two marriages and she died in 19 and 93.

Fonda graduated from Truett-McConnell College as a music major. She and her husband, Allen Riley, are music ministers at the Kennesaw First Baptist Church.

6

COMFORTING THE BEREAVED

Over the 70 years of my ministry I've been involved with what I estimate to be about 1,700 funerals. Some ministers have said that is more than any other preacher from these parts, but I really don't know.

I just always tried my best in funeral services not to say to people what would bring back memories the family didn't want to think about. I just talked to them about more pleasant things. Of the 1,700 funerals I've had every one was a new experience. The different families I've served in endeavoring to help them with their grief and sorrow always felt special.

Back in the early days there were some funeral directors in Gainesville, but we wouldn't call them up here. Embalming in this area didn't begin before the late '30s. There was always a man in the community that dressed the dead. He washed them and dressed them, and laid them out. At that time family and neighbors would sit up all night. Neighbors would come in, some would leave at midnight and others would take their place. There was always a carpenter or two in the community. They'd gather on the front porch and by the light of lanterns they'd make the coffin out of pine wood. They'd always have to come in and measure the corpse to see how long to make the casket and how wide. They'd first line that casket with quilting cotton. Quilting cotton had been ginned and pressed down into about an inch thick in a big sheet. They'd line that casket with that cotton and then cover that with satin.

They'd have to make a top for the coffin and put thumb-screws in each end of the top to screw it down. I remember going to a funeral and the same man that washed and dressed the body would be at the funeral. This was before embalming so the body odor would be setting in and he'd have a bottle of perfume in his pocket. He'd get someone to help him take the lid off when it comes time for viewing the corpse. He'd set the lid aside and then he'd take that little bottle of perfume he had in his pocket, open it and sprinkle perfume all around the corpse to keep the odor down. When they got through viewing, they'd screw the lid back on and take the casket out to the graveyard where some men had gathered and dug a grave.

They didn't have backhoes back then to dig a grave, so it would have to be dug by hand. First they'd go down about four feet. Then they'd come in about six inches on each side and on each end, and dig down two more feet. Then to put the casket down they'd have to cut two 2' x 4's and lay them down on the bottom of that vault, which is what they called the lowest, narrow part of the grave. The 2' x 4's were put in place to keep the casket off the dirt. So after they let the casket down, they could pull out from under the casket the bands they used to lower it. Then someone would have already prepared the covering for the vault. One man would get in the grave, stand on each side of the narrow ledge above the vault, and they'd hand him planks that would reach as wide as the grave was above the vault. They'd lay those planks all the way across the casket and they'd come back and double the planks to cover all the cracks. Then they'd start throwing dirt in the grave.

In 19 and 33, when I first began to be called to assist on funerals, there was an old mountain preacher that pastored White Creek Baptist Church. His name was Lindsey Garner. He was a great old man. I learned some things from him because when he'd get up to preach a funeral he would always call his congregation his children and say, "Now children, there's going to be an empty chair at the table, there's going to be a vacant chair around the fireside."

I would set there thinking, "Well, Brother Garner, they already know that and that's what's burdening them so bad."

I never read much Shakespeare, but I've read a little. And in the little I've read Shakespeare said, "He that saith words to me that are heavier than my grief, does not diminish my grief, but adds to it."

I tried to always use words that would diminish grief.

I remember so well the first funeral I ever had. I had begun my ministry in January of 19 and 33 and this was in October of that year. I had a neighbor that was Mrs. John Head; she had raised a large family. Her husband had died and all her children had married off. She was a rather religious lady because her dad was a Baptist preacher. She wanted me to come live with her to help look after her and keep her company. So I did. The night she passed away me and the family were all gathered around her bed. Back then there were no electric lights and I held the lamp while she passed away.

The family asked me to have a part in her funeral. One of her sons, Doc Head, lived in Cleveland and attended a Baptist church there, so they invited his pastor to have the funeral and I would assist him. But the Baptist preacher never spoke to me when we met at the home about having any part in the funeral. We carried Mrs. Head to the church – Pleasant Hill Baptist Church on Pea Ridge Road – and since I had been staying with the family, I just set down with them at the service.

The pastor preached for about 30 or 40 minutes, and then as he closed his remarks he said, "I understand there was a Preacher Dorsey that was to have something to say in this funeral, but he hasn't arrived yet. If he has then let him come forward."

So I got up and walked to the pulpit and he kept holding on to the pulpit and looking at me. Finally he set down. It's easy for me to remember that first funeral and what an embarrassing thing that was for me.

I had a tent meeting in the Asbestos Community in the fall of '33. Brother Westmoreland was living in Asbestos at that time and passed away. The family requested I have a part in the funeral at Loudsville Methodist Church along with the pastor of that church. We met at the home, but the Methodist preacher didn't say anything to me about a part of the service. So when they took the body out of the hearse, I just stepped up beside him and was going down the aisle.

He looked at me and said, "Now what part of this service do you want?"

I said, "Well, if you prefer, I'll just go up and sit in the pulpit."

He said that was fine with him, so I just set there as he had the funeral. We went to the cemetery, and he did the closing and the obituary.

The family come to me afterwards and said, "What in the world happened?"

I explained to them that it seemed like the Methodist preacher didn't care about me having a part, so I just set up there with him. That's a funeral I've never forgotten.

Then there was a funeral at the Holiness Church over in Murrayville, Georgia, and another preacher asked me to have the first part of the service. I went up without asking him what scripture he was going to use. I read the first six verses of the 14th Chapter of Saint John which starts with, "Let not your heart be troubled; ye believe in God, believe also in me. In my Father's house are many mansions: if it were not so, I would have told you. I go to prepare a place for you."

Then I made my closing remarks and sat down.

The other preacher got up and said, "Now Brother Dorsey read my scripture. I don't know anything to do but read it to you again. He read it again and we both talked on the same scripture. That taught me a lesson from then on – when I was the first preacher and other preachers were to follow, I'd ask them what scriptures they were going to read.

That reminds me of a funeral I had over at Chattahoochee Baptist. A lady that I'd known all my life, Dicie Alexander, that first married a Dillard, and then after he passed away she married Marlin Alexander. She was living with her daughter in Habersham when she passed away. I went the night before the funeral to Whitfield Funeral Home in Cornelia to meet the family. I told them that since the pastor of Chattahoochee would be one of the speakers and likely be with the family, I'd just meet them at the church. I went to the church the next day and her body was lying in state.

I was waiting for the family to arrive. After I had viewed the body, a lady with a pencil and pad of paper come up to me and said, "Brother Dorsey, what scripture are you going to use?"

I told her.

She went back out and when the family arrived and the other preacher got out of his car she asked him what scripture he wanted to use. He told her the same scripture that I'd give her.

She said, "No, you can't use that because Preacher Dorsey is going to use it."

He said, "You go tell Preacher Dorsey he's got plenty more and I don't have."

So here she come telling me I couldn't use that because the pastor was going to use it.

I said, "Why sure, the Bible's full of them."

For another funeral this preacher was to have charge and I was to assist him. At the funeral home he never did mention to me anything about the service so when we got over to the church I asked, "What part do you want me to have?"

He said, "Brother Dorsey, we're just going in there and obey God."

I thought that was a little strange for a Baptist minister, but I said, "Fine, that suits me."

We went into the church not knowing what I was supposed to do. They opened with a song and he got up and read some scripture. He usually talked about 30 minutes at a funeral and was very emotional, but he just talked for about 10 minutes and sat down.

They sang another song and I didn't know nothing else to do but I got up and did my part. When I closed I didn't know what the other preacher was going to do, so I didn't turn the service over to the funeral directors. But the funeral directors was accustomed to when I had the last part of the service, as soon as I set down, they would come down and get the body and roll it out to the hearse to carry it to the cemetery. So here they come and they never looked up at the pulpit.

They started to turn the casket to leave and the other preacher said, "Brethren, I'm not through yet."

So they had to stand there while he preached for a while more. That funeral director said after that he gave that other preacher a talking to.

Another funeral I'd like to mention that was a little odd. I believe it was in 19 and 42. There was a young man that lived out near Turner's Corner that got killed a-cuttin' logs. His mother was a very religious person. She asked me to have the funeral and wanted her son buried in a cemetery just beyond Turner's Corner, next to a church that I think is abandoned now. We gathered at that church, it was a cold winter day and they had nothing but a little heater there. I was preaching the funeral and trying to say something to comfort the family. His mother got happy and went to shoutin' and here come the funeral director, trying to quiet her down.

I told him, "She's all right, she's just rejoicing. You don't have to bother with her."

When we went to the gravesite, there was no grass, just red clay around the grave. They did have a few chairs and a tent.

I read some scripture then said, "Well now, we'll bow our heads and have the benediction."

The mother spoke up and said, "No preacher we won't. We're going down on our knees, and we're going to have a prayer."

I looked down at that red dirt, but I had to kneel in it and ruin a suit of clothes. She prayed for a good little bit.

Brother Claude Hood was a Baptist minister that had a great many funerals, and he and I always worked together so understandingly. He was the type that never would plan anything 'til he got to the church. One funeral we had together was for a lady that lived in North Carolina that died of cancer after a drawn-out affliction. Her husband was named Conley Hefner. He was Robert Hefner's brother. She had written out her funeral and Claude Hood was to preach it because he had baptized her, and I was to assist him. The pastor of the church was to open the service with scripture and prayer. When we left the funeral home and got to the church, we unloaded the body.

As we went up the church steps Claude Hood said to the pastor, "Now you'll have the opening scripture and the prayer."

He looked at Brother Hood and said, "I won't do no such thing."

Brother Hood did not reply, but as we were going down the aisle he pulled my coat sleeve and asked, "Would you have the opening scripture and the prayer?"

I said, "Yes, I certainly will."

So just on the spur of the moment, not thinking that I'd be called on to have the scripture, I asked the Lord to direct me to something. The third chapter of Revelations, the fourth verse come to my mind, where the angel was speaking to the church in Sardis and said, "Thou hast a few names even in Sardis which have not defiled their garments; and they shall walk with me in white: for they are worthy."

When I quoted the scripture the family just went all to pieces. I wondered what did they get so tore up about?

I found out later that Sister Hefner, during her last year, would take walks in the woods. So when I said, "shall walk with me in white," it made the family think about her last days.

Then I quoted the next verse, "He that overcometh, the same shall be clothed in white raiment; and I will not blot out his name out of the book of life, but I will confess his name before my Father, and before his angels."

I went ahead and made my remarks. Then Robert Hefner, Felton's brother, and his singers was doing the singing and they got up and sang, "I want to stroll over Heaven with you." Of course that was a song seldom used at a funeral.

After the service a fella come up to me and said, "Boy, you really had this thing planned out. You read the scripture that said 'Walk with me in white,' and then they got up and sang, 'I Want to Stroll over Heaven with You.'"

I didn't tell him, I just let him think that we did plan it. But they didn't know what I was going to read and I didn't know what they were going to sing.

Back in my early ministry, there were many, many days when I had two funerals in one day, and one Sunday I had three funerals.

We used to have a quartet. I was the bass singer in it. We never practiced, we sang only at funerals. We was called on an awful lot to sing at funerals. Larry Pilgrim was one of our singers and he was good. And then Guy Jones and Marcell Howard sang alto. We'd get called nearly every week to sing at a funeral somewhere. We sang at a funeral at Old Zion Methodist Church, which is now a Lutheran Church. This was in the '40s when there was a Methodist preacher in the area named Nicholson. The family wanted Brother Nicholson to preach the funeral and us to do the singing. Church and Son had the funeral and we gathered at the church. When the funeral hour come we started singing, but the preacher was a little late. Well we sang and sang and the preacher never come. He didn't live too far from the church so someone jumped up and went to his home. He'd forgot about it.

They brought him to the church and he walked down the aisle, sat down, and said, "Let's have a song."

We didn't know nothing left to sing so we turned though the songbook and there was one we found called "I'll Never Move Again," and we sang that.

7

WEDDINGS

I remember the first wedding I had was Did Jones and Ida
Satterfield. My dad was Justice of the Peace and he could marry
people. This was in '34. I was ordained in '33. As we all went to
church on Wednesday night and we was walking down a pathway
that led to a branch and big spring where a big oak tree was at the
head of the spring, dad said to Did, "Asa here can marry you, he's
an ordained minister."

Did said, "Fine, that would be all right with us."

I asked Did, "When do you want to get married?"

He said, "Right now."

The moon was shining bright. It was the fall of the year and I
said," We'll go on down to the spring and we'll stop there and
we'll have a ceremony."

I remembered enough about a wedding ceremony to marry
them. So that was my first couple to marry which was by a spring
under a big oak tree at night under the moonlight.

Another unusual wedding I had was in later years. I had a
knock at my door one day. I went to the door and there was this
fella from over in Kinsey Town. I noticed he was in his pickup and
it had a load of house things on it.

He said, "Asa, I want you to marry me and my woman."

He had gone up to get his woman and loaded up her things. They started home but he wanted to stop and get married on the way. So I invited them in and they got married.

I married a number of couples here in our house and I remember one morning a man was knocking on my front door. It was a stranger I had never seen before. He asked me if I was Preacher Dorsey and I told him I was.

He lived in Lula and said, "You've been recommended to me for counseling."

I invited him in and we went to the study. He looked like he was in his late 20s, or could have been 30.

He said, "My wife and myself are getting a divorce."

I asked, "Is there no chance of reconciliation?"

He answered, "No, there's no chance."

I said, "Well, can I ask you a personal question?"

"Sure," he said.

"How many times have you awakened in the morning and thought, 'Well now, what can I do today to make my wife happy?'"

He looked at me and said, "I've never thought of such a thing."

I told him, "All you've thought of is what she's going to do to make you happy and that's the reason you're getting a divorce."

I talked on with him and had a prayer with him, but I don't know if he still got a divorce.

One Saturday night a couple come to get married, Odell Helton and Betty Holcomb. I asked for their license because I didn't think that Betty was old enough to get married. In those days, when a girl was under 18, the parents had to sign for them to get a marriage license.

The license said she was 18 and I commented, "Well Betty, you've grown up overnight."

It turned out Odell just fibbed a little to get the license. I went ahead and performed the ceremony. Betty was Frank Holcomb's daughter and Frank was a rather high-tempered man. He got the word that Betty and Odell got married so he went and swore out a warrant for Odell for kidnapping. The sheriff come and locked Odell up. He spent the first night of his marriage in the White County jail.

The next morning was Sunday morning. Odell's dad was Alec Helton. Alec was not an educated man, but he was a hardworking, honest man. He got someone with a car to bring him up to Frank's house and they told him Frank had gone to church down at White Creek. So he goes down to White Creek Church. The custom was in those days that the men would gather outside the church and talk awhile before they went in. A bunch of men were standing with Frank when Alec got out of the car and started up to the group. Folks say the group sort of scattered because they knew Alec was a high-tempered man and Frank also. They were afraid there was going to be trouble.

I thought Alec used some mighty good wisdom. He asked Frank, "Frank, if your boy was in jail you'd want to get him out, wouldn't you?"

Frank answered, "Yes, I guess I would."

Alec said, "Well Frank, my boy's in jail."

They say Frank dropped his head for a minute and then raised up and said, "Well Alec, we'll just go get him out."

They both went to the White County jail and got Odell out. Odell proved to be one of Frank's favorite son-in-law's after that. And I married three generations of Heltons starting with Odell and Betty.

One of the hurriest-up weddings I ever had was in '46. At that time I owned the farm that I had purchased from Joe Loggins. I was over there one day plowing with my team of mules in the field

THE GREATEST OF THESE

about 200 yards off the road. I seen a car coming. It stopped and a man got out. He come bouncing across the plowed ground. He was all dressed up and as he got closer, I recognized that it was Clyde Turner.

Clyde come up and said to me, "Asa, I want to get married."

I answered, "Fine Clyde, when's the date of the wedding?"

He said, "Right now."

"I'll have to go change my clothes."

"I ain't got time," said Clyde.

So I just pulled my mules down to the end of the field and tied them. There was a rental house there. I told Clyde to drive the car with Jewell, his bride to be, on out to the house. We knocked on the door and I asked the lady that come to the door if I could use her living room to marry a couple?

She looked sort of strange because she saw I didn't have on marrying clothes and my shoes had red clay on them. I tried to clean them off the best I could before I went in the house. We went in and the lady was the only witness to the wedding. I remembered enough of the wedding ceremony to get them married. That was in 19 and 46 and they're still together today, for which I'm thankful.

8

THE GREATEST OF THESE

In the 13th chapter of First Corinthians, the 13th verse, it says, "And now abideth faith, hope, charity, these three; but the greatest of these is charity."

I put charity, which is divine love, above any other activity. I've tried during my experience as a minister to manifest that.

I remember a young preacher coming to my mill one day and he said, "The trouble with you old preachers is you don't preach on faith, you don't exercise faith."

I said, "Well let's see what the Bible says about that. First Corinthians, chapter 13, verse 13, says, 'Now abideth faith, hope, charity, these three; but the greatest of these is faith.'"

He said, "No, that ain't what it says. It says the greatest of these is charity."

I answered, "Well, why don't you preach it like that?"

He never did say nothing else.

I think churches should do more charitable works to help the needy. Some of the churches today want to build buildings instead of practicing charity.

At Christmas, if I'd made a little money at sawmilling I would buy several bags of flour and crates of oranges and candy enough to divide out among several families. On Christmas Eve night I would get in my truck and I'd go to what I felt was needy families. I wouldn't knock on the door, I'd park far enough out from the house where they wouldn't hear the truck. I'd tote maybe a half a bag of flour and I'd give some sugar and lard and streaked lean meat and soup beans and a crate of oranges. Then I'd go on to the next needy family. I don't know and I don't care if they ever knew who brought it. The next day they could go out on their porch and find it. I didn't do that to think that it would save me, but I did it because I was saved and had the love of God in my heart.

Real charity is giving the last that we got. That was the widow's mites; she gave all that she had. It says in Luke, chapter 21, starting with the first verse: "And he looked up and saw the rich men casting their gifts into the treasury. And he saw also a certain poor widow casting in thither two mites. And he said, Of a truth I say unto you, that this poor widow hath cast in more than they all: For all these have of their abundance cast in unto the offerings of God; but she of her penury hath cast in all the living she had."

I believe in paying tithes, but I also believe that charity comes first. I left the Congregational Holiness Church over the issue of compulsory tithing. I did not agree when they passed the compulsory tithing rule. I believe many preachers today put too much emphasis on tithing. Tithing should be volunteer, not a manmade rule. I come out of the Congregational Holiness Church when they made the rule you couldn't have a voice in the operation of the church if you didn't tithe. It's more important to help those in need, or practice charity. Charity never faileth, but the Bible never says that about tithing.

In John's writing of his First Epistle, in the 3rd chapter 17th verse, he says, "But whoso hath this world's good, and seeth his brother have need, and shutteth up his bowels of compassion from him, how dwelleth the love of God in him? My little children, let us not love in word, neither in tongue; but in deed and in truth."

It didn't say a word about paying tithes, but dividing with your brother in need. So that's the reason I put charity above tithing. I pay tithes but I give to the needy too. I don't give it all to the church.

We read in Christ's ministry he only mentioned tithing twice that I remember in the four Gospels. Once in the twenty third chapter of Matthew in the 23rd verse where he said, "Woe onto you, scribes and Pharisees, hypocrites! for ye pay tithe of mint and anise and cumin, and have omitted the weightier matters of the law, judgment, mercy and faith; these ought ye to have done, and not to leave the other undone."

And then the other place that he mentioned it was in I believe the 18th chapter of Luke starting with the ninth verse: "And he spake this parable unto certain which trusted in themselves that they were righteous, and despised others: Two men went up to the temple to pray; the one a Pharisee, and the other a publican. The Pharisee stood and prayed thus with himself, God, I thank thee, that I am not as other men are, extortioners, unjust, adulterers, or even as this publican. I fast twice in the week, I give tithes of all that I possess. And the publican, standing afar off, would not lift up so much as his eyes unto heaven, but smote upon his breast, saying, God be merciful to me a sinner. I tell you, this man went down to his house justified rather than the other: for every one that exalteth himself shall be abased; and he that humbleth himself shall be exalted."

That's a dangerous thing – to feel that you are righteous in your own self. Righteousness comes from Christ being at the center of our lives, not ourselves.

You have to watch out for manmade rules in a church. I think the reason for so many rules regulations and doctrines is men seeking power over others, to rule the life of others and not trust them to follow the Bible themselves.

The Congregational Holiness Church had a lot of rules when I joined, and I remember well the strict discipline that was enforced by the pastors. That discipline said no one who belonged to oath bound secret societies could be a member of the church. No one that practices lottery or games of chance, or goes to ball games, or picture shows could belong to the church. No one that used tobacco in any form could hold church membership. Women were not allowed to wear makeup. If a member of the church broke any of the rules the pastor could dismiss them from the church unless they repented.

In second chapter of Colossians, starting with the 20th verse, it says: "Wherefore if ye be dead with Christ from the rudiments of the world, why, as though living in the world, are ye subject to ordinances, touch not; taste not; handle not; which all are to perish with the using; after the commandments and doctrines of men? Which things have indeed a shew of wisdom in will worship, and humility, and neglecting the body; not in any honor to the satisfying of the flesh."

Ordinances are rules. That scripture tells me that ordinances – and when a church says you can't do so and so, that's an ordinance – are scary. I decided in later years just to go by the Bible as I understood it, and if the Bible didn't back it up I wouldn't practice it. That throws out so many doctrines and rules.

In 19 and 75 I left the Congregational Holiness Church and became an Interdenominational Holiness Preacher. In January of '76 I rented the old Zion Methodist Church off Georgia highway 115 to have meetings and preach. The crowds began to be so large there that we couldn't seat the people. I contacted the

Superintendent of the Methodist Church about buying the church, but it didn't work out. So we decided to build a new church. In 19 and 76 we built a church – Zion Interdenominational – three miles east of Cleveland on Highway 115, and I pastored there for 10 years. Commissioner of Agriculture, Tommy Irvin, came for the opening service and spoke.

Though I'm no longer associated with the Congregational Holiness Church, I believe in Holiness and remain a Holiness preacher. Holiness should be a way of life directed by the presence of the Holy Spirit. Holiness comes from the Bible. John Wesley taught Holiness and sanctification as a second work of Grace. The first act is being saved, or borned again. Sanctification is a progressive work all through our Christian life, but it has to have its beginning. Nowadays you don't hear many people teach about the beginning of sanctification.

In the 15th chapter of St. John, it says, "I am the true vine, and my Father is the husbandman. Every branch in me that beareth not fruit he taketh away: and every branch that beareth fruit, he purgeth it, that it may bring forth more fruit. Now ye are clean through the word which I have spoken unto you."

Sanctification is the progressive cleansing of the desires of the flesh as it says in First Thessalonians, the fourth chapter: "For this is the will of God, even your sanctification, that ye should abstain from all fornication. That every one of you should know how to possess his vessel in sanctification and honor."

Sanctification gives us power to resist, and helps us have victory over the desires of the flesh, but it's something we have to experience continuously.

In my early ministry as a Holiness Preacher I had rocks thrown at my tent meetings and someone tried to set my tent on fire. There was a lot of opposition to Holiness from the Baptist and the

Methodist preachers when it come to these mountains, and a lot of that was over speaking in tongues. Holiness teaches that an indication that someone has received the Holy Spirit in their life is evidenced by the gift of speaking in tongues. In the Old Testament in the 28th chapter of Isaiah, the 11th verse, it says: "For with stammering lips and another tongue will he speak to this people."

In Luke the 24th chapter, the 49th verse, after Christ has risen from his grave and is giving instructions to his disciples, he says, "And behold, I send the promise of my Father upon you: but tarry ye in the city of Jerusalem, until ye be endued with power from on high."

Then, of course, in the second chapter of the Acts of the Apostles, we see what that power is. Beginning with the first verse it says: "And when the day of Pentecost was fully come, they were all with one accord in one place. And suddenly there came a sound from heaven as of a rushing mighty wind, and it filled all the house where they were sitting. And there appeared unto them cloven tongues like as of fire, and it sat upon each of them. And they were all filled with the Holy Ghost, and began to speak with other tongues, as the Spirit gave them utterance."

In the 10th chapter of the Acts, beginning with the 45th verse, it says, "And they of the circumcision which believed were astonished, as many as came with Peter, because that on the Gentiles also was poured out the gifts of the Holy Ghost. For they heard them speak with tongues, and magnify God."

Then in the 19th chapter of the Acts, starting with the second verse: "He said unto them, Have ye received the Holy Ghost since ye believed? And they said unto him, We have not so much as heard whether there be any Holy Ghost. And he said unto them, Unto what then were ye baptized? And they said, Unto John's baptism."

Then in the sixth verse of the 19th chapter of the Acts, it says,

"And when Paul had laid his hands upon them, the Holy Ghost came on them; and they spake with tongues, and prophesied."

But it warns us in the 13th chapter of First Corinthians that the gift of tongues and other spiritual gifts are of little worth without charity. It says, "Though I speak with the tongues of men and of angels, and have not charity, I am become as sounding brass, or a tinkling cymbal. And though I have the gift of prophecy, and understand all mysteries, and all knowledge; and though I have all faith, so that I could remove mountains, and have not charity, I am nothing."

The 14th chapter of First Corinthians, it's interesting to me about the gift of tongues, it says: "Follow after charity, and desire spiritual gifts, but rather that ye may prophesy. For he that speaketh in an unknown tongue speaketh not unto men, but unto God: for no man understandeth him: howbeit in the spirit he speaketh mysteries. But he that prophesieth speaketh unto men to edification, and exhortation, and comfort. He that speaketh in an unknown tongue edifieth himself; but he that prophesieth edifieth the church. I would that you all spake with tongues, but rather that ye prophesicd, for greater is he that prophesieth than he that speaketh with tongues, except that he interpret, that the church may receive edifying."

I think a heap of Pentecostal people are so selfish they want that self-edification and forget all else.

I want to talk some about God's Grace and how it can change your heart. Grace is the great and mighty gift from God, and it is indeed amazing. Grace is unmerited favor. God is abundantly good to us to give us Grace, when we do not deserve it. We cannot obtain Grace by works or good deeds, we simply must humble ourselves. We rejoice and find hope through Grace. When we realize that God's goodness is extended to us, it elates us. Grace is not only a gift, it teaches us. For in the Epistle of Paul to Titus it says in the second chapter, starting with the 11th verse: "For the grace of God that bringeth salvation hath appeared to all men. Teaching us that, denying ungodliness and worldly lusts, we should live soberly, righteously, and godly, in this present world."

So that tells me Grace is a teacher.

And as it says in the second chapter of Ephesians, starting in the eighth verse: "For by Grace are ye saved through faith; and that not of yourselves: it is the gift of God. Not of works lest any man should boast."

I went to the Holy Land and Rome in 19 and 72. In Rome I visited the Church of the Stairs where Martin Luther once was. People used to go up those wooden steps on their knees until their knees would bleed. Martin Luther was there on those stairs doing penance when God spoke to him and said that being justified by faith through Grace we have peace with God. Martin Luther got up from his knees and walked the rest of the way up those stairs. He later went and nailed his theses on the door of the church and started the Protestant reformation based on the idea that by Grace ye are saved through faith.

Being saved by God's Grace changed my heart toward blacks. I naturally inherited a hatred for black people, but when I got saved, that left me. My dad was very prejudiced against black people. He was a member of a Methodist church, but when a white woman brought in a child she had by a black man to be christened and made a church member, my dad called for his letter. He wouldn't stay in that church because of that baby. He brought the letter home, put it in his trunk, and he never did join another church. I've preached in black churches and learned that there was no difference, only the pigment of the skin.

PHOTO
GALLERY

Camp Meeting, Union Grove Congregational Holiness Tabernacle
date unknown

Rev. Dorsey in his first year of ministry
1933

Asa Dorsey in 1935

Buford Skelton and Asa Dorsey at
Asa's first tent meeting in 1933

Asa and Annie Kate
at Belle's Isle in
Detroit, Michigan
1937

Watson Sorrow and
Asa Dorsey
1936

Rev. Dorsey baptizing in the Chattahoochee River off Georgia 115
1941

Rev. Dorsey and Annie Kate
1943

Ollie Turner, a charter director of Peoples' Ban[
at cashier's window making the first depos[
194

Asa Dorsey on opening day at Union Grove
Congregational Holiness Church
1948

Rev. Hugh Trapp baptizing in the Chattahoochee River off of Georgia 115 after a revival with Rev. Dorsey 1946

Opening day at the new Union Grove
Congregational Holiness Church
1948

Homecoming at new Union Grove Congregational Holiness Church
1948

Opening day at Union Grove Congregational Holiness Church
1948

Opening Day at Union Grove Congregational Holiness Church
1948

Dedication Day, Cleveland Congregational Holiness Church
1950

Union Grove Holiness Campground Meeting
1951

Union Grove Holiness Campground Meeting
1951

Union Grove Holiness Campground Meeting
1951

115

Union Grove Holiness Campground Meeting
1951

Dinner on the grounds at Union Grove
Holiness Campground Meeting
1951

Union Grove Holiness Campground Meeting
1951

Union Grove Holiness Campground Meeting
1952

9

BUILDING CHURCHES AND SEEING HIPPIES SAVED

I've spent 71 years in the ministry of the Gospel, and I trust in those 71 years that I did a bit of good and been of some help to some people.

I've preached in churches in Georgia, Florida, South Carolina, North Carolina and Alabama. The churches I've pastored include Union Grove Congregational Holiness, Mt. Carmel Congregational Holiness, Cleveland Congregational Holiness, Asbestos Congregational Holiness, Helen Congregational Holiness, Welcome Congregational Holiness, Gainesville Congregational Holiness, Nicholson Congregational Holiness, Pentecostal Chapel Congregational Holiness Church in Oglethorpe County, Habersham Mills Bethel Temple Congregational Holiness, and Zion Interdenominational.

I've also preached at camp meetings that include Union Grove, Shingle Hollow in North Carolina, Pirkel Memorial in Griffin, Piedmont Alabama, Glen St. Mary in Florida and the Holiness Baptist Church in Dublin. Some of those had attendance of up to 2,000 people.

I've helped raise money to build churches and taken chickens for donations. One woman I went to see offered me a chicken to help pay for a stained glass window in a church. We was sitting on the porch at her home and she told me to catch me a hen, so I stood up and took off running after one.

I heard her cry out, "Oh, no preacher, not that one, that's my best hen!"

I called back, "That's the one I want, the best you have!"

And that's the one I got.

One of the most interesting churches I helped build was the new Union Grove Tabernacle. I was on the campground committee and one night I had a vision. I was sitting out under the old tabernacle and I looked out and the broom sage was waist-high all around that place where there was once beautiful beds of flowers. I looked down and my hands were so wrinkled that I realized I was old.

A voice spoke to me and said, "If you had done your duty this wouldn't be like this."

I got up the next morning with the determination to see the building of a new tabernacle completed. The campground committee asked me to go around to the churches in the North Georgia District of the Congregational Holiness Churches and ask them to support the new building project of the tabernacle.

I went to one church on a Sunday night and asked them to support the building of our new tabernacle. The pastor got up and announced that the trouble with the churches now was they were wanting to become too much like the world – to be modern. He said they would not be supporting the building fund for the new tabernacle; the old one was good enough.

I went home thinking, "Who am I to be asking people to give to the building program?"

I decided I would not ask any more churches for donations.

But that night, a man come to me in my sleep and told me to

read Haggai, chapter two, verses eight and nine. Next morning the first thing I did was to get my Bible and read these words, "The silver is mine, and the gold is mine, saith the Lord of hosts. The glory of this latter house shall be greater than of the former, saith the Lord of hosts; and in this place will I give peace, saith the Lord of hosts."

When I read these words, I decided to finish what I had been asked to do.

The price of the tabernacle, that was 100' by 150' come to $21,500 erected. We had the old building torn down by Roy Gerrells and his boys. We got Bob Palmer and his crew down there working along with Phillip Palmer and Hoyt Tomlin, and we had to dig the footings. Being 100-feet wide in steel beams, we had to have a three-foot anchor on each side in concrete. Then we had to go from one side to the other, dig a trench, pour 12-inches of concrete and put steel rods in the concrete to match up to the pillars we would put in. We started pouring the footings.

Buford Skelton and I were standing down at the southwest corner, looking across to the north corner, and he said, "Brother Dorsey, this looks just entirely too big. We better cut it down while we can."

Remembering Haggai, chapter two, verses eight and nine, I said, "Buford, this place will be running over the first Saturday night. I can raise half the money to pay for it the first Saturday night."

He responded, "If you can raise $9,000, I'll give the tenth."

After the tabernacle was erected and the first Saturday night of camp meeting arrived, we couldn't seat the people. They were lined up three deep all around the outside of the tabernacle.

Buford was careful to remind me, "You said you was going to raise the money."

I answered, "All right, I'll give it a try."

I got up and in seven minutes I'd raised $8,000. Then here come a little boy running up to me with part of the back of a song book tore off.

It said, "Sit down, shut up, I'll give the next thousand." It was signed with initials, "CCB" which was Clifford C. Blalock.

Buford Skelton gave the next thousand so we collected $10,000 the first Saturday night of camp meeting in 1961.

One of the churches I had pastored before, I was elected to pastor again in the fall of 19 and 72 – Union Grove. That was the time of the hippies. In my evangelistic work I traveled down to Martin's Crossroads, which is between Lincolnton and Augusta. Several times in revivals I got acquainted with some families down there. One of the families sent two of their boys – one was a hippie and one was saved – to North Georgia Trade School to further their learning. So they heard about me pastoring at a church and they come to that church and the other one got saved. They began bringing others with them, and the first thing you know, we had a crowd of hippies with long hair, and their knees out of their trousers, and their toes sticking out of their shoes. Some of them didn't smell like they'd taken a bath in a month. But I just preached the Gospel to them. Two of my deacons didn't like it because I was letting those hippies come to church. One by one they began to get saved.

One old boy from New York, he was the hippie leader and all he knew was the hippie talk. He come to the altar the first Sunday and just knelt there. But the next Sunday night he come back to the altar and started praying. I walked over to where he was kneeling at the altar to pray with him.

About the time I got over there he fell back on one elbow and raised his other hand in the air and said, "Preacher, I'm high tonight."

And that was a different high then what he'd been accustomed to. I continued to preach to them the Gospel message, I didn't say anything to them about their clothes. I had a lady from a former church I'd preached at come to my house and told me she wanted to talk to me. We went in the living room where we could have some privacy and she began to tell me that she didn't approve of what I was doing.

She said, "I hear that you have this bunch of hippies attending your church, they have long hair and ragged clothes. I'm surprised in you. You know the Bible said if a man has long hair it's a shame to him. They tell me you haven't said a word to them hippies about the long hair!"

I replied, "Well, when I used to be your pastor at Asbestos, it was in the early days, about 19 and 39 and 40. The girls had just begun to bob their hair, cut their hair off shoulder length. You began to holler that bobbed hair was wrong for them. You said the Bible tells us that if a woman has long hair it's her glory. I remember some preacher come out and made a song about that. Part of one stanza was, 'Why do you bob your hair girls? You know it must be wrong. God says you must wear it, and you must wear it long.'"

Then I told her, "You called those ladies that had their hair cut shoulder length bob-haired girls. Now when is your hair long, and when is it short?"

She didn't give no answer.

One Sunday I walked in the church and there was a young man sitting on the back seat. They called this boy "Old Bill." That's all I ever knew him by. On this Sunday the young man was dressed up and had on a suit.

I asked some of the others, "Who's the young man in the back?"

They said, "That's old Bill, he's cleaned up and got a haircut."

The best I remember there were a great number of converts of those hippie boys that come from the trade school and got saved. All of them finally cleaned up, but they still used some of their hippie language. They'd get up and testify and refer to their girl-friend as "my chick." That was a new expression to all of us. Out of these young men, there was four that became ministers of the gospel.

We had a baptizing in Lake Lanier where old Highway 129 crossed the iron bridge. Old Bill was in that group. When I baptized him, he come up out of the water and took off swimming. He swum a long way out into the lake then he come back. As I led the candidates out of the water he joined in. That's the only candidate I ever had that took a swim after baptizing.

10

ANGELS AND MIRACLES

I've witnessed, and experienced miracles, and I believe in angels.

God from the beginning of time has had a ministry of angels. In the 16th chapter of Genesis, when Sarah had given up on having a child and got her maid, Hagar, to have a child with her husband, Abraham, we see that an angel spoke to Hagar.

It says in the seventh verse, after Hagar had fled Sarah because Sarah became angry, "And the angel of the Lord found her by a fountain of water in the wilderness, by the fountain in the way to Shur."

And the angel said to her, "Hagar, Sarah's maid, whence camest thou? And whither wilt thou go?"

And she said, "I flee from the face of my mistress Sarah."

And then the angel said, "Return to they mistress and submit thyself under her hands. I will multiply thy seed exceedingly, that it shall not be numbered for multitude. Behold, thou art with child, and shalt bear a son, and thou shalt call his name Ishmael; because the Lord hath heard thy affliction."

So we see angels can speak to us.

In the first chapter of Matthew, starting with the 18th verse, it says, "Now the birth of Jesus Christ was on this wise: When as his mother Mary was espoused to Joseph, before they came together, she was found with Child of the Holy Ghost. Then Joseph her husband, being a just man, and not willing to make her a public example, was minded to put her away privily. But while he thought on these things, behold, the angel of the Lord appeared unto him in a dream, saying, Joseph, thou son of David, fear not to take unto thee Mary thy wife: for that which is conceived in her is of the Holy Ghost."

I was driving home late at night after a revival in South Georgia in 19 and 58 when I actually felt the presence of an angel so much that I felt over in the passenger seat to see if a person was there. It was about 1:30 a.m. at night and I was coming up Bells Mill Hill, driving an 88 Oldsmobile. All at once I seen a cow in the road, almost like a mirage. I slammed my brake on so hard my guitar come into the front seat with me. I always felt like there was an angel protecting me that night because I was running at a high speed and could have easily had a serious accident, but I didn't.

The New Testament is full of stories on the workings of miracles. Not only Christ did miracles, but also Paul and the Disciples did miracles. I have seen miracles in my own life.

I remember in 19 and 37 we had come back from working in Detroit Michigan and were living in the David Dorsey home in White County. I had a funeral the next day. There was a rising on the back of my neck that was so severe that I couldn't turn my head. In my family prayer that night I asked God to heal my neck so I could at least turn my head the next day at the funeral.

The next morning, we got up, and while having our morning prayer, the Spirit said to me, "Feel your neck."

I felt my neck back there, and it was as smooth as it is now. That was a personal miracle.

In 19 and 42 we were having a revival at Union Grove. Naomi

Forester, who was John Forester's wife, had four children and her last child left her bowed over. She couldn't straighten up and she went that way for about a year. She come to the revival one night and we were having prayer for those who wanted to pray and needed to be healed. I saw this with my own eyes, we prayed for Naomi and she straightened up, as straight as she was when she was a young lady. She remained straight until her death. She was in her '90s when she passed away.

I had a good customer at my mill and I heard he was in the hospital in Gainesville. Of course at that time I visited the hospitals as a minister at least twice a week and sometimes three times. I went down to Northeast Georgia to visit him and found him to be a real sick man.

He told me, "Preacher, they're going to have to send me on to Atlanta. They say they can't do the surgery I need here."

One thing I learned in visiting is to make my visits as short as possible because when you're hurting, it's easy to get tired of a visitor.

I never knew of him going to church so before I left I called him by his name and asked him, "Are you a Christian?"

He answered, "No, I'm not."

I asked him, "Would you like to be?"

He said, "Yes, I would."

I gave him a few Bible quotations about how to receive the Lord by believing and accepting Jesus as his savior.

I said, "Now as I pray, you pray, and just tell God how you feel in your heart. That's what God wants to hear from all of us, not a fancy prayer, just how you feel in your heart."

So we prayed, and after prayer he'd picked up a little.

I asked him, "Do you feel better?"

He answered, "Yes, I do."

I said, "Well do you feel like Jesus saved you?"

He said, "Yes, I do."

I then left with the knowledge that he was going to Atlanta the next day to have some very serious surgery.

On the third day from that, I was back at the hospital. The folks that worked at the information desk down in the lobby, they'd gotten used to my visiting. They'd usually hand me the list of names that was in the hospital and I'd look them over to see if there was anyone I knew. I seen his name back on the list.

I thought, "Well that's strange."

I went up to his room and he was looking so different from just three days before when he thought he was dying.

I asked him, "Well how are you feeling?"

He answered, "I'm feeling fine."

I said, "Tell me about your operation."

"I didn't have no operation," he explained. "But let me tell you a story. They'd scheduled me for surgery for eight o'clock the next morning, and they'd already taken X-rays. But later that night a nice-dressed young man walked into my room. He was the kindest-talking young man I ever heard and I just enjoyed talking to him. After we'd talked a little while, he turned to leave and when he got to the door, that young man looked back, called me by my name and said, 'You won't have to have surgery no more.' Then he was gone. Early the next morning they come and wheeled me to the operating room."

The surgeon come in and said, "I want to take another picture of this man before I do the surgery."

"After they took the X-ray, I noticed two or three doctors were over there looking at that picture. Finally, the surgeon come over to me and said, 'Your problem has disappeared over night, you don't have nothing to operate on.'"

My friend then asked me who I thought the young man was?

I told him that it must have been an angel, and I thought of the scripture in the book of Hebrews, chapter 13, the second verse: "Be not forgetful to entertain strangers: for thereby some have entertained angels, unawares."

He come home the next day from the hospital.

As I said earlier I had the misfortune of going broke in the chicken business in 19 and 53. We had built a feed mill in 19 and 51 and took on a franchise with the Ralston Purina Company. We started putting out baby chicks all over the county and a few in Habersham County. But the bottom fell out of the price of broilers in the later part of '53 and the first part of '54, and I had no other choice but to declare I was broke. I was advised by some friends to declare bankruptcy, but I told them, "No, I won't do that."

Most every day over the next few months I received statements reminding me that my account was overdue. I must say it kept me doing everything I could to keep my creditors satisfied. One day a letter come in and I noticed the return address was from Dr. L.G. Neal, our family doctor. As busy as I was, my wife would just have to carry the children to the doctor when they needed to go. I paid Dr. Neal if not monthly, then whenever I got the money. I think I had run up an account with him in doctor bills of about $300, best I remember, which was quite a bit of money back then. I opened his letter and to my surprise here's what it said: "Dear Asa, in recognition of the good that you have done in White County, and in my greatest appreciation for your ministry, I'm marking your account paid in full."

That was the only creditor I had that gave me my account. In later years, after he had retired, I heard Doc Neal was in the hospital in Hall County and I felt obligated to go see him. He and I had become real good friends. He was in the end room. His wife was sitting in a chair by the window just to pass the time, watching the traffic.

She said to me, "Asa, the doctor won't know you; he hasn't known any of us for two or three days, but I appreciate you going in and speaking to him."

So I went in and spoke to him and he opened his eyes and called my name. That was a surprise to me, and to his wife, too.

My daughter, Miriam Vandiver, was one of the nurses at Northeast Georgia Hospital then, and Doc Neal happened to be her patient. She entered the room about that time. She had a habit of laying her arm around my neck and asking me how I was doing.

Doc Neal said, "Well there's Marty."

He called her Marty; a lot of people do. So I just stepped back against the wall and let her do her work. By that time Doc Neal's wife had come in and was standing on the other side of the bed weeping like a baby. When Miriam left the room, Doc looked at me.

He said, "Asa, who's that there behind you?"

Doc Neal had a way of parabolically speaking about things. I thought maybe he meant who followed me pastoring the Holiness Church in Cleveland. So I responded by saying, "Doc, you mean who followed me as the pastor for the Holiness Church in Cleveland?"

"No." he said. "Who is that standing there right behind you now?"

Of course, I was so close to the wall I didn't look around, but I felt like he saw an angel standing there.

The next day he passed away.

11

THROUGH THE EYES
OF FRIENDS AND FAMILY

Tommy Irvin, Georgia Commissioner of Agriculture: I was born in '29 and raised in White County. We were sharecroppers that lived in the area from Woodlawn over to Leaf. I went to school one year at Woodlawn, and also at New Bridge, but most of my elementary schooling was at Chattahoochee School. I remember as a child we'd go to the Holiness campground at Union Grove for summer revival. They had little cabins out there and it was a genuine camp meeting. Brother Dorsey would either preach in the day service or at the night. Best I can recall they'd have at least two or three evangelists to carry on that revival. I know my Granddaddy Watt Hogan never would sing, but he'd always sit in the choir and clap his hands right in tune with the music.

We didn't have a car so we'd hitch up the mules to the wagon. We grew our own wheat for our bread and if we had a little extra straw we'd put it in the bed of the wagon and we'd put a quilt over it. Ladies back in those days would make quilts. When we got to the campground we'd tie the mules up. Some folks had horses, but daddy always believed in mules. In those days revival would go on sometimes after midnight. Nobody was really in a hurry to go home. Coming to camp meeting was the highlight of the year. We were all farmers then and at that time of year, most folks had already laid their crops by. Camp meeting was a real social event and we'd go there to meet girls.

When church was over at night and we were ready to go home, we'd untie the mules, all lay down in the wagon bed, and go to sleep. The mules would wake us up when they were home in the barn lot.

P.S. Dorsey and my daddy both worked at the sawmill together. Asie worked there some too, but he was so busy in those earlier years preaching. He probably preached more revivals and funerals than any other preacher in Northeast Georgia. And my father was one of those funerals. We moved from White County to Habersham County when I was 16 years old and that was the year daddy got killed at a sawmill in a work accident. It was around 1946. We carried daddy back over to White County in a truck; the roads were all dirt back then. There was never any doubt about who would do the funeral service. We had great respect for the Dorsey family and we all considered Brother Dorsey our minister. Daddy's buried at Chattahoochee Baptist Church there in the Leaf community. My mother's buried there, too.

Everybody had respect for Brother Dorsey. If people don't have respect for you they'll shy away. It's not so much your ability to preach, it's the life you live. And I think the life that Brother Dorsey lives is what sets him apart from so many other ministers. Everyone I know that ever knew him has absolute respect for him. He has a beautiful voice with great delivery. When he preaches, he really understands the Gospel. He could take a message, decipher it, and present it in a way that few others could do, and people would understand it. He could preach at a level that it wouldn't go over their heads.

At one time he worked for me as an inspector. I don't mind

saying when we first started talking about him going to work for me, some of his children had some reservation about him working for the state because inspectors have to enforce laws. And if you enforce laws sometimes somebody may get mad at you.

We had this man over in Lumpkin County who just had total disrespect for our burial laws for chicken houses. You have to build a poultry pit and you have to keep all your dead chickens there. That law was in effect when I became commissioner and I enforced it. We had this man that wouldn't keep his pit up. You have to dig a hole in a certain shape and if you don't service it, it will cave in on you. The inspector that we had been sending over to check on this farmer lived in the community, but the farmer would run him off with a gun.

We decided to see if Brother Dorsey could get him to comply. Of course we totally briefed him on the all the circumstances. Brother Dorsey went to this farmer's home to try to meet the man and get him to fix his poultry pit, short of us having to take some legal action. Running off our folks with a shotgun was pretty serious.

The wife of this farmer opens the front door and recognizes Brother Dorsey from preaching so many revivals.

"Brother Dorsey, come right in, I'm so happy to see you," said the woman. "We've been hoping you might pay us a social visit."

Brother Dorsey takes off his hat and walks in. The woman explains that dinner is on the table and her husband would be in shortly from working on the farm.

Brother Dorsey was able to get her to calm down and let her know that he was there on some official business. He tells her he works for the Department of Agriculture and he's there to talk to her husband about being uncooperative with his poultry pit.

She said, "Don't you worry about that, I can handle that. Whatever you want him to do, I'll see that he does it. Let's just forget about that, we want to socialize."

He took care of business. He took a hostile situation and turned it into a joyous occasion. That's the man. He can take a dangerous situation and turn it into simple compliance. He also had a very positive influence on the other state employees he worked with because they had so much respect for him.

The Zion Church that he founded was a great success and he invited me to be there and say a few words for the opening. I really enjoyed being there that day and on the other special occasions he invited me to attend because it gave me a chance to see old friends I grew up with. Brother Dorsey gave me a beautiful Bible with my name on it when he was pastor of Zion Church. I used that Bible for many years until my daughter gave me a new one. His ministry has touched so many lives in these mountain counties.

Carol Jackson, Georgia Senator: I'm grateful that it was part of God's plan that Asa Dorsey touched the families of White County and Northeast Georgia the way that he has. His life has enriched the lives of many other people, not only through his ministry, but also through his family. One of his son's, Bradley, was my classmate. I knew all of his children growing up, and not only did he live an exemplary life, but he and his wife, Annie Kate, taught his children to do that. His life, his ministry and his family will not only influence his generation and his children's generation, but also generations to come.

Asa conducted the funeral service for both my grandparents – Anna Carroll Campbell and Jamie Campbell. He did an outstanding job at their funerals. Asa has a gift to say the right thing at the right time whether it's a tremendously sad occasion such as a funeral, or a time of happiness like a wedding or a birth. He has an absolute calling to know and say the right things that people need to hear at a special time.

I brought his name before the Georgia Senate for a resolution because I can't think of a more deserving person. Having lived as many years as he has, and having set such an example for so many others, and having given so much to the community, it was only fitting and proper that he be recognized. The members of Georgia's General Assembly need to lift up role models like Asa who contribute so much to make our lives better. I know in my lifetime that Asa Dorsey has prayed for me and my family, and so many other families in these mountains. I know he has prayed for the leaders of Georgia and our country. We know that the founders of our country, when writing the U.S. Constitution, took time out to pray for divine guidance, just like our leaders need prayers for guidance today. The life and ministry of Asa Dorsey have helped us all and I'm thankful the Georgia Senate resolved to show appreciation for his contributions. He's a remarkable man.

Shirley McDonald, historian and columnist for the White County News & Telegraph: My family was from the Asbestos community and my granddaddy, Bart Black, had lived there all his life, near where Asa put up his first tent. All Grandfather Black's nephews, like Barnett Blalock, lived up there. Barnett's mother was a Black; she was my grandpa's sister.

My grandfather went to his grave blaming the Holiness for burning down the Mt. Yonah School in Asbestos. Some Holiness members had asked to borrow the school to have a meeting there, but they would not let them use it. It was locked up. Well, the school burned and my grandpa always blamed the Holiness folks. But I've learned and I now think it was an accidental burning and it wasn't the Holiness that did that. But everybody was suspicious of them back then because it was a different religion. They could go to church in their overalls, they didn't have to get dressed up.

People weren't used to hearing banjo music in church, and the Holiness would shout and talk in unknown tongues. They were definitely different. I remember older people talking about it, saying, "it was the work of the devil."

I wanted to go to their church because I was curious. I remember hearing that they would take you by the hand and pull you down to the altar, so I made sure I sat on the end next to the wall in case it happened to me. But those things were made up because people didn't understand Holiness. It wasn't true, but you know if that's what you hear, that's what you believe.

Seeing and hearing Asa Dorsey preach made me think that there was more to it than what I'd been hearing because he was such a fine-looking man and always so calm and quiet. He always blessed me when I heard him preach. I think he's responsible for the Holiness growing in these parts.

After they built that little church next to Ollie Turner's yard, Ollie was so good to them. They would have revivals that would sometimes go for a week and last four to five hours up to midnight. People would go out to Ollie's house to drink water. My parents wouldn't let me date until I was 16, but you could still go and eye the boys over there. I remember Paul Elliott playing his banjo. That was entertainment back then, there was no television and not many places to go.

I worked nearly 35 years for the health department and I remember a widow whose house burned down and her neighbors telling me that it was Asa Dorsey who was out contacting people in the community, organizing to get help, both monetary and furnishings, for that lady. He was the Red Cross back then.

One day I was at Northeast Georgia Medical Center and a woman there realized I was from White County. She told me her daddy was raised in White County. He died when he was in his 30s from cancer, and they had had a hard time because he couldn't work and her mother had to look after him. They had actually gone without food in order to get her daddy's medicine.

They went to the drugstore one day and the druggist said, "You get all this medicine – the bill is already taken care of."

Her mother asked who was helping them, but the druggist said that information was asked not to be divulged. It was many years later that she learned it was Asa Dorsey. He went about doing good without bragging about it, and it didn't matter what religion you were. I don't think there's a family that lived here prior to 10 years ago that hasn't been touched by Asa Dorsey. I've never heard one person say a harmful word about him. He has a personal touch that most people don't have; I think that's a gift.

He did my husband's funeral. Though my husband did not belong to a church he really respected and admired Asa Dorsey. I'm sure that's who he would have chosen. Asa did a wonderful job comforting us. You couldn't have asked for a nicer funeral.

Aubrey McIntyre, business owner and pastor: Brother Dorsey was asked to take part in so many funerals because he knew the people as well as anyone in White County and surrounding areas. He was just a master at picking the right scripture and saying the right things. People would come to a funeral downhearted, but by the time he finished his ministry, they were uplifted, and not so much in despair. They had a reason to be happy that their loved one was going to a better place. Asa has the ability to just do that. He was gifted with a great voice, his words were so well-pronounced, and he had a great vocabulary. The tone of his voice would captivate your attention. Other ministers could say close to the same thing, but they wouldn't get that word in there like Asa did. His voice was so commanding that it would hold your attention; it was deep, it was not too overpowering, it was just right. People didn't go to sleep on Asa, they listened to what he had to say. And he was a great storyteller. At a funeral he would always come with a story for the family that would pick them up.

The way he handled his creditors when he went broke revealed that he was a true Christian. He worked through all that and demonstrated that he was just the kind of man that would live up to his obligations. With the integrity he showed in his life it was not even necessary for him to sign on the line; he'd stick to an agreement whether he had a contract or not. He was just that sort of man.

His life was an example to others; he set a pattern that others wanted to use as their standard. Ministers of all faiths and denominations have admired him so much, not just as a pastor of a church, but his everyday life. They wanted to be like him; he was their role model.

He put good people around him starting with Annie Kate, his wife. I remember his telling the story about someone in the community that was down on their luck. He told Annie Kate, "We ought to get some things together and take them some food, or maybe some clothes."

Annie Kate said, "Asa, I've already done that."

This makes for a better man when he has a great companion.

He was also real involved with getting churches started in the community. He brought income in to help churches from places where you wouldn't necessarily look for it.

He would just go tell the people, "We got a need for building this church to honor God and God's people." And they would rally to the cause.

He lived with charity in his heart. Asa taught tithing, but he didn't teach it from a mandatory standpoint, and neither do I. It's so much better to present it as a blessing of tithing. He taught it from the blessing side rather than putting straps on people, saying if you want to be part of this church you've got to tithe. We are our brother's keeper and owe a helping hand to our fellow man.

Though Asa was appreciated by the upper echelon of society, he tended to lean more toward the less fortunate people. He had compassion in his heart and he is loved by others. There's not a greater man in White County than Asa Dorsey.

Eunice Jones, schoolmate and singing partner: I went to school with Asie at Woodlawn, and I've knowed him all my life. I'm 84 years old now. We always called him "Asie." The school we went to was a different Woodlawn School than his dad had bought. My husband was Guy Jones and we was good friends with Asie and his wife. Guy farmed, and sawmilled, and he worked at Cleveland Lumber Yard. He also worked down at Lays Potato Chips in Chamblee, and we lived there for a while. Asie's father married me and Guy at his home. We were members of Union Grove, but my daddy, C.H. Autrey, was a Methodist preacher. He gave the land for that church and I was little when that church was first built. We lived right out from the church. All that land in front of the church is where we farmed. Me and Guy used to farm on that land.

I enjoyed going to tent meetings. We had a quartet and used to sing with Asie. He was good at quoting scripture from memory; people would follow him in the Bible and he don't miss nothing hardly. He's good at preaching funerals, if he's still alive I guess he'll preach mine. He's a very kind person.

A lot of people was just against Holiness when it started; they would tell tales on Holiness. They thought back then that Holiness folks would put powder on you, turn out the lights, and look for Jesus. Guy's mother, she went to hear a Holiness preacher,

Preacher Duncan. She didn't want to go, but she went anyway. She got happy and went to shoutin'.

Camp meeting was different from what it is now. The meeting would start in the morning and it hardly would ever close. They'd start praying about seven o'clock in the morning. Some would pray near the altar and some would go out in the woods. People would start shoutin' after they were praying and singing. At night they'd start at about eight o'clock because people had to farm. They'd sing, and sing, and sing. Then the preacher would preach about two hours. People didn't get tired like they do now and the singing was so much better than now. Camp meeting was an important part of mountain life. When people farmed they could come to camp meeting at night or church and be with their neighbors. That's the way me and Guy met – we always went to church and Guy did too.

Nella Jones, daughter of Eunice and singer with Rev. Dorsey on the radio: I think Asie's so good at funerals because he knows everybody and knows stories about everybody. When he preaches a funeral it's not just a sermon, he really goes into their lives. He's interested in other people and truly cares about them.

In the old days there were no phones and no cars to go no where, so coming to church and camp meeting was an important thing. Everybody in the community was there. You found out who had married. Back then the whole choir was full, hundreds of people, and they'd sing 'til the power was felt.

We used to travel around and sing. My dad and my sister, Myra, and I, we'd sing with Asie. He would preach at different churches. My other sister, Helen, would play the piano. We had a radio program in Gainesville with Asie. We'd sing at seven a.m. in the morning and Asie would preach. Myra was the lead singer, I sang alto, daddy sang tenor and Asie sang bass. Helen played the piano. The theme song was "I got up this morning feeling fine, I got up with heaven on my mind."

Asie believed in practicing charity; he had a lot of compassion for others. He preached this past October from First Corinthians on charity. If you only pay tithes to a church, you may lose sight of the needs of the common people. If you see a person in need, maybe God allows you to see that person. If you just pay your tithes to the church you may say, "I gave my tithes, I don't need to help that person." Helping others is what makes a better community.

Ann Jackson, employee of Rev. Dorsey: I became acquainted with the Asa Dorsey family in the '50s because I went to school with Asa's daughter, Trilla. We went to school, church and youth camp meetings together.

My father, Verner Pilgrim, worked for Asa at the feed mill. I remember daddy coming home covered with corn meal and feed where they had ground corn at the mill. Sometimes he would be late for supper. Although they closed the mill at six p.m., daddy had to make sure the money came out to the penny because he did not want to cheat anyone out of anything. They would go over and over the receipts for the day until they could find the error. So I guess I knew that Asa Dorsey was an honest and good man from my daddy.

In 1962, I went to work at the feed mill office helping keep the receipts. Asa taught me about weighing the trucks with loads of corn, then weighing when they were empty. I learned how to balance the checkbook and send out bills to customers. It was always stressed by Asa to treat everyone alike, and never to cheat anyone out of anything. He would send me to the bank to make a deposit when I was only 16 years old. To me that meant a great deal; it showed me that he trusted me with his money. I learned from him that if you can trust people you don't have to worry what is going to happen next.

Rev. Dorsey's wife, Annie Kate, was my mother's best friend. To my family she was like an angel. Many times Rev. Dorsey and Annie Kate would travel to different hospitals in Atlanta, Gainesville and Habersham County to visit our mother, father, brother and other members of our family who were sick and dying. They always came with a prayer, an uplifting song, a quotation from the Bible, and usually a good cake to eat. Annie Kate could make the best cakes. We considered them our adopted family. They helped us through some very hard times.

And now I work for Rev. Dorsey again, staying in his home with him during the daytime. Rev. Dorsey is the same every day, offering a smile, a kind word, a hug, or a pat on the back. He loves to talk about Jesus in everyday language. I enjoy listening to him tell great stories about the '20s, '30s, '40s and '50s. You cannot begin to imagine what an incredible memory this man has. I am so thankful to be able to share in hearing his memories. He's one of God's treasures on this earth.

Garland Lovell, childhood neighbor of the Dorsey family:
The man is the closest to being a second daddy to me as anybody has ever been. I have so much respect for him. Our families go back and intermingle since day one. He was a savior to our family. The summer that I was 11 my daddy had a terrible sawmill accident. I guess what Asie did for us could be considered charity, but he didn't make it feel like charity. He gave me a job when I needed a job.

Me and Thandal were the same age, and we did about every job you could for him – chasing chickens, digging ditches and foundations for chicken-houses, and hauling grain out of Tifton,

Georgia. One summer he hired me and Thandal to clean out layers of chicken litter. He contracted with us to clean out a chicken house at ten cents a load. We went at it all day and finished about dark hauling loads. He came in and asked us how many loads we'd hauled out. We told him about 40.

He sort of gave his chin a rub and said, "You boys are spending too much time driving back and forth from the chicken-house to the pasture."

Well, that night he put 16-inch sideboards on that equipment we were using to haul the litter. But that's the way he was; he demanded efficiency. Those values he taught me while working for him gave me a sense of responsibility and helped me every day as a management supervisor. They affirmed what my momma and daddy were trying to teach me.

He's a very religious person, but never forced his religion on anybody. He lived by example. He never arm-twisted me to become a Christian. His life just said this is what being a Christian has done for me, but you make your own decision. On sunny days it's easy to be a Christian. When he went broke, that probably tried his soul more than anything else. But he lived by a creed like my mother and daddy and many who went through the Depression. They were a tough bunch of people with a tremendous sense of morality and responsibility. He would have done anything to be sure you got back every nickel you were owed. He would never cut a corner.

I felt comforted when I was just around Asie. He's done all the funerals for our family. There's something about him, that if you looked up and saw him conducting a funeral, it just felt so natural and good. Anybody who has never met the man has experienced a loss.

Helen Farmer, childhood neighbor of the Dorsey family and sister of Garland Lovell and Debbie Brady: Asie Dorsey cared so much for people. My daddy, Fay Lovell, worked for him and had both legs broke by a tree, and Asie was there for him. He made sure that we were all looked after. That would have been in the late 1940s. Most everybody looked up to him. He was good at the funerals because he knew so much about everybody and how to calm people and make them feel better. That's what he did at both momma's funeral and daddy's. If something happened to me that's the man I'd want to preach my funeral. He married me and Vernon Farmer in the living room of his house 43 years ago last January.

You had to love Annie Kate. She was the sweetest, best person I ever knew of; there was nobody else like her. When our sister died, she and Thandal come that evening and stayed with us until 11 o'clock that night. She treated everybody the same.

She was a great cook and made beautiful cakes. She's the one that told me that you didn't have to use certain measuring cups to bake just so long as you used the right ratio that was needed. She had a peanut butter jar that she used to measure her flour and her sugar. She made such big cakes and they were so good I just paid attention to what she said. I always tried to make my cakes like hers.

Asie was good friends with my grandfather, Jessie Lovell. Asie was baptized in my grandpa's fish-pond. Our house was just below the pond. That's where we used to chase snake doctors. Snake doctors is what we called dragonflies because wherever they buzz around, there's a snake nearby.

Asie's boys played ball over in our field all the time. A road is all that separated our property. We were neighbors, and I've spent many a night over at their house. Growing up under my grandfather and Asie Dorsey you didn't get in a whole lot of trouble. My grandfather was a deacon in the Holiness Church.

Debbie Brady, childhood neighbor of the Dorsey family and sister of Garland Lovell and Helen Farmer: Asie Dorsey was a role model, and so was Annie Kate. Annie Kate was like a second mom to me. If something had happened to our mom I believe we could have gone over there and she would have been the mother to us that she was to her own kids. She was always the same; nobody was different with her. Fonda and I were the same age, and we were together a lot.

When our mother died recently my first thought was, "Where's Asie? I need for Asie to hug me. I need to be around him."

He always knew who you were; he always remembered you, and it didn't make any difference how many years it had been. It was his way that made you feel comforted. There was no other person on this earth that we could think of that would be better standing up there talking about our mother. There's no one else that you want. You can tell it's very hard when it's someone really close to him. He tears up but it's not put-on tears; it's genuine. The many lives he has touched shows that he was sent by God.

When Asie was preaching, he would walk from one end of the stage to the other and never look at his Bible. He knows scripture so well. If you needed anything, all you had to do was ask, and he would do his best to help you.

The story about him going broke and calling together all his creditors and not declaring bankruptcy but paying them back tells you about the person he is. Being the kind of person he is, that was the only thing he knew to do. And his children turned out really well; they are pretty close to what he and Annie Kate were. They were taught they had to work, and it didn't hurt any of them.

Melanie Partin, niece of Garland Lovell, Helen Farmer and Debbie Brady: I have strong memories about Asie and my grandfather praying together. All the kids would be at my grandparents' house, and Asie and my grandfather would be in the kitchen on their knees praying. My grandfather, Fay Lovell, was a very quiet man. He and Asie were very similar. He would come in, sit in his chair, and read the Bible.

What strikes me the most about Asie is his deep compassion, and he's just always so humble. You could be there squalling at a funeral, and the stories he tells about your loved one that just died are so comforting. He even tells stories that make you laugh during a funeral. When my grandmother died, he told stories about when he married my grandparents. And then he was there for the end of their lives by doing their funerals.

He was always helping people. Even when the cows would get out because the pasture fence was torn down, he would come help you repair the fence. I used to go to his feed mill; it was always busy. The values of his life were the same values in his business. His word was as good as 10 million contracts. If he told you he would do something, you could take it to the bank.

Young people today could learn a lot from the way Asie treated people and wanted to help others. He would have given you the shirt off his back if you needed it. Those are values of true Christianity. It's better to see a sermon then hear one. A lot of people talk the talk, but Asie talks the talk and walks the walk. He lives the lessons of Christ.

You could tell Annie Kate was also a humble loving person. Both of them just had this spirit about them – such a giving, comforting spirit. They were role models for a lot of the community – the way they raised their children and how they helped others. People were drawn to them; there was just this magnetism.

Charles Allison, business owner and pastor: I preached a few funerals with Asie and always looked forward to working with him because he was so knowledgeable about the Word. He pastored a lot of churches around, and a lot of people knew him. He told me once that every funeral was different and he treated them all special. The reason he had so many funerals is he was so great at scriptures and touching people with his words. Everybody wanted him because he was so good at it. The Lord gave him a gift – when he would go to minister, the scriptures would just come to him almost like he was reading them. That was a gift from God.

Sue Allison, attended many of Rev. Dorsey's tent meetings:
We all called him "Asie." He's respected by people from all walks of life. His life has touched so many other people's lives. His ministry has to be a gift and a calling from God, because you know funerals are not pleasant, and he just has a way of showing love. That has to be placed there by God.

He can use words so well, and it's not great, swelling words. He's a quiet and meek person, but the way he portrays the love of Christ, through living for him, and the life that he has lived for him, it just comes out. Asie lives what he preaches and people can sense the love in him.

He has respect for people. He knows your people, and that just shows. His memory is so amazing, he remembers people from way, way back and who their children are. He was a friend to all my kinfolks around Turner's Corner. We moved up near Turner's Corner when I was about five years old.

My grandmother was Pentecostal from the New Holland Congregational Holiness Church down at Gainesville, Georgia. My mother, Nelle Jackson, got acquainted with Holiness through my grandmother. People up here didn't know too much about that back then. To them it was a strange thing.

I liked going to his tent meetings. Tent meetings is all we knew back then. Living at Turner's Corner, it was like living 50 miles from Cleveland. They had tent meetings on our land where the garden is now. They would also hold them by the old Corbin Store, right across the road, and at Oscar Cannon's. The Holiness preachers like Asie would visit a lot in your homes. When I was a child they would haul us all the way to the Holiness Campground. I've seen a lot of men bad to drink get saved, and their life was different from then on. Holiness people believed in cleanliness; they believed God could take care of your habits like cursing and tobacco, anything like that.

I remember my Aunt Zora Jarrard, when she hadn't fully gone into Holiness. Aunt Zora made her home with us; she was like my second momma. We was sitting on the old porch out there and the camp meeting was just up the road. Aunt Zora had her little thing of snuff. I can see her 'til this day. She'd just take that snuff and dip down in it and she'd use it. Well, church was getting ready to start and Aunt Zora couldn't get enough of that snuff. She told me it was the best snuff she'd ever used in her life.

She said, "Well, I tell you what I'll do. I'm going to set this snuff up right here and when I get back from church, I'm going to get my fill of it. That's how good that snuff is."

She went up to church and got a blessing from God, and Aunt Zora never used snuff again.

Holiness was disliked. There was opposition to building the Welcome Holiness Church near my home. They found that some-one had possibly tried to burn the church down. I can remember people would throw eggs and do other ugly things. But that never stopped us. We never said anything harmful to nobody, we just went on. A lot of opposition came in around the doctrine of once saved, always saved. We reject that. The Holiness believed in living up to what the Bible says about sanctification. People like Aunt Zora could be delivered by God's grace. People aren't taught that as much now as back in those days. Your life is a process of growing in Grace.

But people from other denominations loved Asie. I think it's because of the life he's lived and what he's portrayed to people, like his honesty. There's just something different about him that has to be of God. He uses whatever scripture God lays on his heart. His words can make a picture and people just enjoy it. You can feel the spirit in him. And he's always been a neat person, neatly dressed, and you just look up to him.

Ross Palmer, pastor and peer of Rev. Dorsey: The reason Asie Dorsey is so unique and such a great minister is because God wants someone that will listen to him. In the Bible days, when Jesus called his disciples, he chose the unlearned so he could teach them something. Asie was like myself, without much education, but God could work through him. God picked Asie, a poor farmer, to run a revival in my home community of Asbestos, and there's never been a greater revival in White County.

There's a little church in Asbestos that Asie founded. My wife got saved there and she come back home. We hadn't been going to church and I'd been running a beer joint right up here by the bridge just above Cleveland. My mother died when I was about two years old. My daddy had to work hard and I didn't know anything about the Bible. My wife said if you'll tend to our two little girls I believe I'll go to the church out here, the church Asie Dorsey started. She come back about 12:30 and walked in with her hands just waving.

I said, "What in the world happened to you?"

She answered, "The Lord just saved me!"

I didn't know what it was all about. The first night she started prayer, her and our little girls got down by the side of the bed. I jumped in the bed and covered my head. I didn't want to hear it. But I couldn't pick a fuss out of her for about two or three months. I was a heavy smoker at the time, and one day I walked out on the porch. I didn't know how to pray, never had read the Bible that I knew of.

I told the Lord, "I don't know how to pray, but just give me what my wife's got."

He did; two years later I was called to preach.

People want him to do funerals because he's got so much compassion, he's so humble. That's what attracts people. I've seen him get up there and not read a scripture through what he'd be shedding tears. He's the most humblest man I ever met.

I heard a story that he was running a revival up in North Carolina somewhere and there was so much power and the spirit of God in the midst that some people standing outside come crawling through the windows. Rural churches back then raised the windows up. They crawled through the windows to accept the Lord.

One of those big conferences they had, a Pentecostal conference, they picked him out to be the preacher. So after he got through preaching, they come to him and asked what seminary he went to, or what college he graduated from, and he said, "I got to the fourth grade."

Me and Asie, we was talking at the funeral home when his wife passed away.

Asie said, "I never heard her raise voice with our kids."

I questioned him, "Well you know why, Asie?"

"Why?" he asked.

I said, "She's a Palmer."

God gave him so much wisdom; he's a very smart man. If anybody brings a subject up he can just start quoting scripture. We were at a funeral home here just a while back and there was two or three preachers standing around there asking him some questions. He'd carry them back to the scriptures in the Bible. He'd quote it verse for verse and then say the next scripture says this, and then he'd go to another place and say the scripture says this. I mean just on and on. I would say he's touched more people in White County than any other preacher that's ever come.

Clyde Turner, business owner married by Rev. Dorsey: Asie Dorsey turned the Asbestos district upside down around 1932-33. He took a following through Asbestos and it ain't never left. He's one of the most thoughtful men in the county. He turned some people where they was drinking and made them whole, and they died whole. There was a lot of drinking going on and that caused a lot of problems. Those were hard times back then. There's no doubt what he didn't turn Asbestos up one side and down the other. He got a following that started then and ain't never ended, and that affected three or four generations.

I wanted him to marry me and my wife, Jewell, so we could stay together through thick and thin. I thought he could join us together and so far he has. He did seal it up good; we've been married since 1946.

He's meant a lot to this county and surrounding area, through his wisdom and bringing the spirit of God. He's the most honest person, A through Z, that I know of.

Mary Shelnut, comforted by Rev. Dorsey's funeral service: He was so comforting; that's what he's about. He has the right words to say at the right time to help people. I think God gives him those words. That's why so many people love him. He has a humbleness that people just feel and sense. He was a pastor at Welcome Church out near Turner's Corner where I was raised. As a child I remember all of his family coming with him to church. Some of his children were my age.

Curtis was my second child, he died at ten months old. I never thought twice about who I wanted for the service. My husband's side of the family knew Brother Asie as well as my side of the family. Everybody sees him as a man of God because his spirit bears witness to your spirit. That's how you can tell who is a prophet and who is not. He's the most loving and humble person, and that's a characteristic of Jesus Christ.

Maebelle Smith, comforted by Annie Kate and Rev. Dorsey: There can't be nobody no better than Annie Kate and Rev. Dorsey. When I would get sick and go in the hospital, they would come. And then the minute I got home they'd fix me a big plate, or a pot of soup, and he and Annie Kate would bring it to me.

Without Brother Dorsey, a lot of people wouldn't have had salvation. And mercy, there was nobody on earth could make a cake like Annie Kate could. She made them for birthdays and weddings, and for anybody that wanted a cake. When my Momma was having her 88th birthday, she made me a cake, a tier cake like a wedding cake and it was the best thing. My Momma just had a fit over it.

When I was in the hospital and they would walk through the door, you could just feel the love. One time I needed some papers that were in my pocketbook back home. They went out to my house, picked up my pocket book and brought it out to the hospital to me. When my son had surgery, Brother Dorsey was right there at the hospital with him. He could just comfort you.

There was a time when I was bad depressed after my husband died. Layman died the 9th of February in '80. I'd get to crying so that I couldn't call Brother Dorsey. So I'd call Trilla at the high school and say I can't call your daddy for crying so bad. Would you call him and tell him I need prayer real bad? You could tell when he was praying for you.

I wouldn't take nothing for the two of them. When she was living I'd go in their garden. They'd call me and tell me to come pick beans if I wanted them, and I'd come pick beans and can them.

Henry Freeman, business owner raised with the Dorsey children: I've known Brother Dorsey all my life. I was raised at the Union Grove Church and went to school with his boys. We played ball together. In those days, Brother Dorsey, he forbid the boys to play ball. We would go to their home on Sunday and eat Sunday dinner and they would come over to our home. We would slip off to the pasture and play ball. Brother Dorsey was always a very strict disciplinarian with his family. I think that discipline helped his kids, and it helped us neighboring kids because of his beliefs. When you look at his family, I don't know any family that's done any better.

He was recognized as a spiritual leader in the community and people would go to him when they needed counseling, before they would go to their own pastor. All walks of life would do that. I've recommended some of my employees to go to him for spiritual advice. He's been a devout man all of my life and I've been knowing him about 60 years.

His specialty was conducting funerals. The last count I had he'd preached more than 1700 funerals. I guess my wife Susie and me sung in 500 or more of them. Going back to my early childhood memories, I remember Brother Claude Hood and Brother Dorsey would preach funerals everywhere. They just had that dynamic charisma that families wanted to hear. Brother Dorsey had a knack for getting up there and comforting people that needed comforting. He's known all over the Southeast.

I understand one time he went to the tax office when Mildred Campbell was the tax collector and told her to raise his tax so he'd be equal to his neighbor. How many people do you know would do that?

I've served on church committees with him and worked with him on building buildings at the campground. He's a taskmaster; he demanded perfection, and demanded people be dedicated to their task. He commanded respect, but on the other hand he gave respect. He was my pastor as a child and as an adult. In those days we didn't have full-time pastors and they had to have a way of making a living, so they had a business of their own, or had to work a job.

Paul Flynn, Rev. Dorsey's pastor at Union Grove Congregational Holiness Church: It's remarkable – his mind is still brilliant, much brighter and more alert than mine is. He has a gift, a way to reach people with the compassion and knowledge that he has. He's been a great role model, instructing me how to stand at funerals so that it's more respectful and comforting to the family. He can relate to families so well; he knows something on all of them that he can tell about and get a laugh even when families are crying. It's a blessing to be able to do that.

In my childhood I had always heard of Asa Dorsey up in North Carolina at a place called Shingle Hollow in Rutherford County. That's where I lived when I first heard him preach. His name was almost worshipped and he was highly regarded as one of the most anointed of Holiness preachers. His preaching was straight without any foolishness; he didn't try to preach opinions, he preached the truth. He used more scripture than any preacher I ever heard. He's known everywhere you go, especially among the older generations, as a minister of the Gospel. He's looked up to because of the life he lived was for Christ. When he went broke, he gave up his license to minister because he thought it could be considered a reproach on the church. To be a good pastor, you have to be a good servant, and that's what Brother Dorsey is, a servant to the people. Brother Dorsey could preach for an hour and make it seem like 15 minutes, while I could preach for 15 minutes and make it seem like an hour.

The Bible says you can't love someone unless you know the love. The Bible also says for a man to have friends he must first show himself friendly. I guess Brother Dorsey has as many friends as there are anywhere. He always wanted to set a standard. The standard of Holiness used to be very strict – no TV, no theatres, no ball games, no shorts, abstain from worldly things. He was strict, and he's told me he'd seen in a lot of things maybe he'd been too dogmatic. But he was trying to set a standard, and he lived by that standard.

When I came here 15 years ago I went to him and invited him to preach. He's been a lot of help to me, and so was his wife, Sister Annie Kate. That lady had the most wonderful smile, even up until when she died. When I preached her funeral I used the last chapter in the book of Proverbs about a virtuous woman and that described her. She was a great help and support to Brother Dorsey's ministry. She was always right there for him. When you walked in a room with Sister Annie Kate you could just sense the virtues she had. There was a spirit of goodness about her and a smile that was all about her kindness and her compassion. She was just different.

I never felt worthy to do a funeral with Brother Dorsey. If I was asked to do a funeral I would always go first. There's no preacher in the country that wanted to go last behind Brother Dorsey; there wouldn't be nothing for nobody to say. He had the love, he had the call, he had the anointing. He was chosen and sent of God. He made great sacrifices in his life to promote the Gospel. He was a minister at a time when there was no money to pay, and he had to walk to preach. Those are things some preachers wouldn't do today. The church has become a place for entertainment rather than worship. Brother Dorsey had a commitment to Christ and he preached that whether people liked it or whether they did not. He's known from Florida to Virginia to Alabama to Mississippi. He was one of the top preachers for camp meetings in his earlier years.

It's been an honor to work side-by-side with Brother Dorsey and learn from the examples he set. He's a gentleman, a born-again child of God, and he's fixing to get his reward. When Brother Dorsey passes from here to heaven, we will miss a great man that leaves a great legacy.

Tye Sorrow, pastor and son of the Holiness Congregational Church founder: My dad was Watson Sorrow and he was the founder of the Congregational Holiness Church; he got it all organized. Brother Dorsey and Brother Buford Skelton were close friends of my dad and they used to come to our house and talk to my dad on scripture and other things. My dad always said Brother Dorsey was like one of his own boys; he held him in very high esteem.

Brother Dorsey has had such an impact on the community. I've known him all my life, he's 12 years older than I am. I pastor the Congregational Holiness Church in Abbeville, South Carolina, and people still mention his name around Abbeville. Rev. Dorsey is known all over.

He was asked to do so many funerals because he was the type of minister that could speak to any congregation of people. He knew when to come with doctrine and when to leave it alone. He had wisdom. He was one that was really called and chosen. Many are called, but few are really chosen.

L.G. Howard, a bishop of the Congregational Holiness Church:
Asa is respected throughout the southeastern United States and is the best known pastor in the Holiness movement, especially among the older members. When I travel in states like Georgia, Florida, Alabama, and the Carolinas, people always ask me, "How is Asa Dorsey doing?"

His daily life bears witness that he's lived what he preached. He's put his preaching into practice in his life. The number of funerals he's been asked to do speaks of people's impression of him as a leader and a minister – the confidence they have in him. I think the number of funerals he's preached is a record in this part of the country. He's been a Christian gentleman all these years. A lot of people have professed a personal relationship with Christ, but he has the goods to prove it. Asa has been a mentor to me; he has helped me far beyond his knowledge.

My mother was Icie B. Howard and my daddy was John M. Howard. We lived in the Asbestos district back then and Asa and Buford Skelton came in and put up a tent. In 1933 my mother was at that tent meeting in Asbestos and she went into a trance. They hauled her home in a two-horse wagon. Garvis Elliott and his family were very much involved in the revivals. He went down to visit my mother one day and asked her if she remembered the tent revival in Asbestos. She said she did and would never forget it. She related to Garvis that the Asbestos tent meeting was a deep spiritual experience that made an impression that lasted all of her life. My mother died in the spring of 1993 a week before she was 86 years old.

Asa has a testimony that he was praying one night before going to bed about this family that had just moved into the community.

They were very poor people and needed help. He was asking the Lord to help this family, to bless them. The Lord spoke to Asa and said, "You bless them; you've got the means."

He went and did what the Lord told him to do.

It didn't matter to Asa what church a person belonged to; it was just the Bible he would go by. If he saw someone was out of line with the scripture he would call their attention to what the scripture says. He would share it with them for their benefit. He's done funerals for people from many different denominations.

Asa didn't have any formal education. He was preaching a revival up North and a lady came up to him expressing her appreciation for the message he'd preached.

She said "I'd like for you to come preach at our church."

"I'd be glad to," Asa replied.

She asked, "How many degrees do you have?"

He answered, "Well I guess you could say four."

"That's great; what degrees are those?" she asked.

"Well I went through the fourth grade in grammar school," he said.

Asa said she never mentioned him coming to preach for her church no more.

Asa's wife, Annie Kate, was a very good person; she was kind, very soft-spoken. A wife can be the making of a good minister. A preacher faces all kinds of things and just because he is a preacher doesn't mean people are always going to be kind to him. Annie Kate was such a help to him in both the good times and the bad.

Asa once told me, "In all of my ministry, my wife has never told me one time she appreciated what I preached. She's always been there with me, but she's never commented."

Annie Kate wanted Asa to be totally led by the Spirit and not impressed by her suggestions.

Asa told me he had a dream one night. He dreamed that he was being robbed. They stopped him in his car; they robbed him; they took his money; they took his clothes; they took his car. They left him naked in the woods and drove off in his car. In his dream Asa saw a light and started walking in that direction so he could get somebody's attention. This man come out of a building – after Asa got his attention – and then he went back in the building. In just a little bit, the police drove up and told him to get in the car.

Asa said to the police, "Look, I've been robbed; they took everything."

The police responded, "Yeah, we know all about that; come on, get in the car."

Asa got in the car, and he knew they didn't believe him. He told them, "I'm a preacher."

The police said, "Yeah, we've heard that story before, too."

"But if I quote you some scripture, would you believe what I'm saying," asked Asa.

"We might," they answered.

Asa started quoting scripture and it just kept flowing.

The police said, "You know, I believe you are a preacher."

Then Asa woke up from his dream.

He told me, "I got to thinking about that and there was a time when the Bible wasn't free for everybody to use. I committed myself to memorizing the scripture. If I got it memorized and they took the Bible from me, they couldn't take it out of my mind."

That's why he can quote scripture so freely – because he committed it to memory.

Rudolph Parton, recalling Rev. Dorsey's ministry in North Carolina: I was about five or six years old the first time I ever met Asie when he came here to our camp meeting at Shingle Hollow in North Carolina. And it was about 1946 that he came and ran a revival at Sulfur Springs. There was a church down around Sulfur Springs, North Carolina that had split – some of the members got the baptism of the Holy Spirit. They started a little church in a house owned by a Mr. Green. That house is still standing and I live in Rutherfordton, North Carolina, about 15 miles from where the house is located. Asie came here and had a revival in that house that lasted about a month. A lot of people got saved and got the baptism. I remember the house was so full you couldn't get in. One man climbed in the window to get saved. I would have been seven years old then but I remember the man came in the window, went up to the little alter and got saved that night. The man's name was Nathan Hinson, and he was a farmer in the community. Some nights that revival would last to one or two o'clock in the morning. Asie basically started a church after that revival called Sulfur Springs Congregational Holiness Church.

I can remember the first loud speaker I ever saw, a public address system that Asie had up on top of his car. He had one speaker turned toward the front of the car and one turned toward the back. He would stay with us at our house a lot when he was up here. He would go to town and play records and invite people to the services. I remember some of the songs he played. That was along about the time the Winecoff Hotel burned in Atlanta, and one of the records he had was a song about the burning of the Winecoff Hotel. I road around with him some and it fascinated me, that loudspeaker system. Then during camp meeting he would set it up to use it for preaching.

His mannerism set him apart from other preachers. He was real soft spoken, just kind of a gentle person, and that attracted you to him. His personality caused people to listen to him. He just had that spirit about him, such a humble spirit. People seeing his life wanted to be Christians. It did me. We've got children here in this community named after Asa Dorsey. Asa Arrowood, a deacon in our church is named after him.

Sharrell Dorsey, oldest child of Rev. and Mrs. Dorsey: You can condense it down to three words. I call it the three "Cs" for courage, commitment and character. Mother and dad both demonstrated these traits every day that they lived. Mother was geared more toward the family – her caring, courage, her character and her commitment to the family were always foremost in her mind. Dad was committed to the family, but his commitments were more to his ministry and the things pertaining to the church and God's work.

One of my earliest remembrances was in 1941 when Pearl Harbor was bombed, there was a lot of activity around the house. People were coming and seeking not only spiritual guidance, but also wanting to be reassured that everything was okay. Looking back, I realize that incident was an indication of mother and dad's commitment to the community, and how the community depended upon mother and dad's moral and spiritual guidance. I think I would have been about five years old at that time.

When one of the neighbor's sons was killed in action the community always called on dad to take the lead in making sure arrangements were made, and a memorial, or some sort of prayer service was held. Mother was right there with him.

Then there was the night in the early '40s that Pledger Boggs and Grant Hooper were killed in an automobile accident. Pledger and Grant were both devout Christian men and would go to work after the Sunday night service. They were working in Atlanta at Atlantic Steel. After the Sunday night service was over they'd gather up their families, carry them home, and then head to Atlanta to be at work that night.

I never will forget this particular Sunday night. I was probably five years old, seeing Grant Hooper pick up one of his boys and sling him over his shoulder. The last I saw of Pledger Boggs was his silhouette going out the back door of the old Union Grove Church. Sometime in the early morning hours of Monday someone came to the house and told dad that both Pledger and Grant had been killed in a head-on collision just south of Gainesville. The great burden of pretty well having to handle all the details of the funeral arrangements and the grief involved, all fell on the shoulders of mother and dad.

I recall after the Saturday afternoon bath that we all had fresh clothes we would put on. We would see mother, especially in the wintertime, out in the wind and the cold, scrubbing and using that old scrub board. Those were the best-smelling clothes you'd ever smelled.

Another early memory was in the early '40s when REA power company ran electricity to our house. That was a very exciting time, the first time that we sat down to the supper table and had a light bulb hanging over the kitchen table so we could see to eat, rather than having a lantern, and worrying about cleaning and refueling that lantern.

In later years I wondered how mother must have felt. First she had to get dad off to work at about 5:30 every morning, then stand by there watching a first grader on his way to school for the first time, knowing there was nothing she could do because she had other children at home to attend to.

I remember during my second grade in school, dad and W.B. Robinson, going to Atlanta to the army surplus store to buy an old white school bus with the capacity for about 20 kids. It was again dad demonstrating what had to be done to make sure the kids had some means of transportation to get to school.

Around 1946 we were building rabbit boxes and every morning

at five o'clock, often in the wet, cold winter, mother would wrap us up and we'd go out to run the rabbit boxes, hoping we'd find some rabbits. Sometimes we found other varmints in the boxes, but most of the time we'd find a rabbit or two. We'd go to the store and sell those rabbits for what seems like a quarter or 50 cents apiece. Occasionally, we'd kill those rabbits and mother would fry them for breakfast. We'd have rabbit with gravy and biscuits.

One of the things that still sticks in my mind is on Sunday morning, mother and dad, packing all of us kids in the old '42 Chevy and going to small churches. We'd journey to these churches, packed in the car in our Sunday best clothes with our hair slicked down, and we'd try to behave. We'd go to Helen, Turner's Corner, Habersham Mills, Cornelia, Alto and to other small churches. Lot's of times on Sunday night it was right back to going to churches.

Union Grove camp meeting was one of the big events of the year and we'd have a little bit of freedom to get up and roam around and be big guys. We had a restaurant there at the Union Grove meeting and I was given the opportunity at about age ten to sell ice cream bars for ten cents apiece. I slipped me so many of those things it almost made me sick.

In the late '40s, dad would pack our '47 Plymouth and I don't know how we made it to Shingle Hollow, North Carolina, with stuff tied on top of it. We would jam in the car and I'm sure we looked like Jed Clampett and his family. Mother and dad had tremendous patience with a car-load of kids and having to travel to the camp meeting in Shingle Hollow. Dad would be one of the main ministers, and we lived in the preacher's cabin. At the Shingle Hollow camp meeting the blacks attended and worshipped along with the whites. The blacks were not designated to sit in the back; they could sit where they chose, and the choir was a racially mixed choir. And this was in the late '40s. That is always something that stuck in my mind as very unique and a great thing.

Home was a place of refuge for a kid. When you go off to school, there's always a bully. Regardless of how tough the day was at school and how scared I got, my thoughts were: "If I could just get home to mother." Home was a place where I knew I was loved, and if I could get home and talk to mother for a few minutes, she could make everything okay. When we would come home, mother would always have something special – biscuits, cookies or tea cakes. But then we had chores and they had to be done by the time dad came home. There was no exception to the rules.

In looking back, one of the things that has amazed me was how mother and dad, and especially dad, would let us assume responsibility such as driving trucks. Of course we were required to do the chores such as milking cows at five o'clock in the morning and feeding the stock. Mother and dad were brought up during the Depression, and it was very, very tough times. You had to be tough; you had to be able to take the knocks; you had to be able to survive. Dad would let us assume responsibility and let us succeed or fail based on our skills and abilities. Lots of times we failed, and we didn't get a lot of sympathy when that happened. We were driving tractors at 10 or 11 years old, and trucks and cars by the time we were 13 or 14.

Miriam Vandiver, oldest daughter of Rev. and Mrs. Dorsey: With dad being a preacher we were raised "going to church." Other than our visits to grandparents, uncles, aunts and cousins, all our social contacts were through the church.

We always had a "family altar" at home, and dad would gather his family for this event every morning before breakfast, and again at night before going to bed. He would read scripture from the Bible and have prayer. We always had to sit still and be quiet during the Bible reading, and we all got on our knees for the prayer.

Occasionally dad would call on each of the children to contribute a few sentences to the prayer. This was usually awkward for us children. Family alter took place every day, and it did not matter if we had friends or guests visiting. They were also expected to show proper respect for the Bible reading and get on their knees with us for the prayer.

Dad was very strict and authoritative in his child-rearing philosophy. The children were not allowed to talk back, or question rules, or what they were told to do. Any indication of disobedience or rebellious attitude was quickly taken care of with a whipping. Therefore, we learned at a very young age to respect and obey our parents.

Most of us don't remember dad being home very much. He was always gone either with his work or his ministry. When he was at home, there was farm work to be done, or time had to be set aside for Bible study and preparation for ministry.

Dad worked hard to provide a living for the family. He had many business ventures over the years, and some were more successful than others. The churches he pastored in those early years had very little money to pay him, so there was not that much income from the church. He oftentimes ended up giving more back to the church, or some in need in the community, than he received.

The children had to learn responsibility and hard work very early in life. These responsibilities came before any playtime. The boys had to do all the farm chores and help dad in whatever way they could in his business operations. On the farm there were pigs to be slopped, cattle to be cared for, cows to milk, chicken houses with chickens to be "grown out," eggs to be gathered and graded, wood to be cut and chopped for winter heat, and various other chores to be done.

The girls were responsible for helping mother in the house.

They had to help care for the younger children, help prepare meals, wash dishes, wash clothes, hang clothes to dry and clean the house. They also worked in the chicken house when needed to gather and grade eggs.

Mother was the one us children spent most of our time with. She was the most loving, caring, nurturing, generous, unselfish person I ever knew. She made our house a home with her love, warmth, kindness, gentle guidance and teaching. She also taught us many things about life and what constituted acceptable attitudes and behavior in the family and in the community. We knew not to do anything that would give us a bad name or bring disgrace to the family. We knew we had a responsibility to uphold the reputation of dad as a minister.

As an adult looking back on childhood I can appreciate the home mother and dad made for us. We knew we were loved. We always had enough food and shelter to meet our needs. We learned by their example; we were taught what it meant to have character and respect. Hard work taught us responsibility and commitment to a task.

Trilla Pruitt, second daughter of Rev. and Mrs. Dorsey: Being the second daughter with four older brothers, I was drawn to the boys and their activities more than my older sister Miriam's routine. My mom always said that I would rather help dad and the boys rather than do house chores. I was pretty much a tomboy.

The memories I have of following dad and the boys around the farm and the feed mill encompassed most of my childhood. My earliest memories of dad relate to the time he was producing chickens and traveling from farm to farm to check on them. The chicken houses were in the community where we lived, and I knew most of the farmers well. They knew dad from his preaching, pastoring and the feed mill. Most everyone respected dad because of the Christian life he lived. Most people really respected mom and dad because they spent a lot of time giving back to the community.

We always respected dad, but unlike many children today, we would not dare tell him how we felt. Dad was a very strict parent, and he expected only one response when he was talking to you. The answer better be either a "yes, sir" or "no, sir." Comments and opinions were not allowed. We were taught that parents were the authority, and children didn't have a voice. Furthermore, we were to listen and follow orders without complaining. The rules were simple: respect adults without back-talk, finish every chore with pride, play without fussing with siblings and friends, and work hard without complaining. Dad grew up without much time to be a child. He left home to work on a dairy farm at around 12 years of age. He had lots of responsibility at an early age, and he raised his children in much the same manner.

Dad's parenting philosophy was to let experience be the teacher. I'm sure that his early responsibilities shaped his parenting beliefs, therefore dad was never one to explain details of a job or chore. He usually gave some general idea of how, or what to do, and then left the rest to the child.

I was about ten years old and always in the middle of the boys and the chores. I really wanted to learn how to drive our farm tractor. One day dad told me I could drive the tractor. Standing a few feet away from the "old Ford," he told me to climb onto the driver's seat and get ready to drive. He was on the ground and gave me a few minutes of instructions, no more than two or three sentences.

"Here's the brake" dad explained, pointing to the brake pedals. "Here's the gas, and here's the ignition. Hold down the clutch, turn the key and remember to let the clutch out easy, give it some gas and guide the thing. That's all there is to it. See what you can do."

The boys were my audience as I was careful to follow the sequence of instructions. With a big jump I took off. I was going way too fast, but I was doing good on the steering. The problem was I ran out of road pretty quick as I was in our drive in front of the house. I didn't know to push in the clutch, but I remembered the brake. However, one minor detail that I did not get was that there were two brakes, one for each wheel. I knew that the brakes should stop the tractor, but I failed to push down both of the brakes. I was so anxious that I stood on one brake, with the gas still way too fast. Needless to say, one tractor wheel was still spinning and digging up dirt, and I was going in circles plowing up the front yard. My brothers were having much fun watching, but I think dad had already walked off. They were screaming for me to shut off the gas. I finally got over my panic enough to react to their screams. When I cut off the gas, the tractor slowed to a crawl, and I was able to push in the clutch to stop the vehicle.

When I finally got stopped, no one had to remind me that the tractor had two brake pedals, and that the gas lever was the most important factor in the whole process. Dad never gave me a lecture. In fact, I don't remember him saying anything. The incident served to teach me that experience is the best teacher, and maybe that I should ask more questions next time. I learned several valuable lessons: (1) tractors are dangerous equipment (2) listening closely to instructions is important and so is asking questions, and (3) trying was part of learning.

I learned to be a very careful person from experiences like these. I think dad's philosophy was that the experience taught me much more than a big lecture could have.

12

THE METHODIST/HOLINESS/PENTECOSTAL MOVEMENT

BY LARRY FRICKS

In the summer of 1990, while a staff writer for the Gannett newspaper, *The Times* in Gainesville, I went on assignment to St. Simons Island to do a story on John Wesley and his early 1700s mission in Georgia.

Wesley is credited with sparking the great 18th Century Evangelical Revival and founding the Methodist and other related denominations that now include some 50 million people world-wide. Among those denominations is Holiness, which Reverend Dorsey was called to serve two centuries after Wesley's death.

At age 32, Wesley came from England to the Georgia coast in 1736 and served as a Church of England chaplain under General James Oglethorpe. He yearned to minister to American Indians, but he failed miserably in that mission and others.

Wesley's ministry focused on two British settlements separated by 80 miles of coast: Savannah and Fort Frederica on St. Simons Island. A museum focusing on Wesley's life and work is now located on St. Simons Island at the United Methodist retreat center named "Epworth by the Sea," after Wesley's birthplace, Epworth, England.

Wesley and his brother Charles were educated at Oxford, where they met with a small group of students who studied the Bible methodically; thus the name "Methodists."

The serious Bible scholars led by the Wesley brothers prayed and fasted together, and visited the sick, the poor, and prison inmates. During his lifetime Charles wrote some 6,500 hymns including the Christmas favorite "Hark the Herald Angels Sing."

Both Wesleys crossed the Atlantic Ocean together to face the missionary challenges in the rough and ready Georgia frontier, but Charles returned to England within a few months.

John Wesley's high-brow, strict and tedious approach to religion was rejected by the Georgia pioneers struggling to hack out a rugged existence while serving as a British outpost to protect northern colonies from a Spanish invasion out of Florida.

Accustomed to great respect for his religious intellect, Wesley experienced failure and the ultimate humiliation when a Savannah grand jury indicted him after he refused to offer the Last Supper sacrament to Sophy Hopkey, daughter of a prominent community leader.

Wesley and Hopkey had courted, but he dragged his feet asking her hand in marriage. She wed another, and Wesley appeared a jealous spurned lover when he refused – because of a church technicality – to offer Holy Communion to her. In late 1737, Wesley fled the grand jury charges in Georgia, never to return to America again.

Back in England, a depressed Wesley was left questioning his calling to the ministry. Besides his melt-down in Georgia, he was deeply troubled by a faith-shaking experience that occurred some two years earlier while crossing the ocean headed to America.

In the middle of the Atlantic, raging storms battered and nearly sank Wesley's ship. During the crisis, Wesley panicked and feared for his life. To his shame, he realized that while his faith in God faltered, a devout group of German families – known as Moravians – calmly prayed and sang hymns during the storm.

"…The Sea broke over, split the mainsail in pieces, covered the ship, and poured in between the decks, as if the great deep had already swallowed us up," wrote Wesley in his diary. "A terrible screaming began among the English. The Germans (looked up, and without intermission) calmly sang on."

"I went to America to convert the Indians," continued Wesley in his diary. "But oh! Who shall convert me! Who, what is he that will deliver me from this evil heart of disbelief?"

In great despair Wesley reached out to a devout Moravian who helped him grasp the concept that salvation is a gift of God's grace through faith, not works.

At a prayer meeting in London at Aldersgate Street, on May 24, 1738, Wesley experienced a climactic spiritual awakening that he described as having his heart "strangely warmed" by God's love.

As written in Wesley's diary: "I felt I did trust in Christ, Christ alone, for salvation; and an assurance was given me that He had taken away my sins, even mine, and saved me from the law of sin and death."

Wesley began to preach with a new power he called "an out-pouring of the Holy Spirit."

Most Anglican churches closed their pulpits to Wesley, and he was frequently persecuted in experiences similar to those of Reverend Dorsey and other Holiness ministers when they first began holding tent meetings and evangelizing in the mountains. Although Wesley was sometimes attacked by angry mobs stirred up by Anglican ministers, an evangelical awakening erupted.

Wesley went to the coal mines where the working class of England were harshly oppressed and began preaching in open fields to them. Historians have credited Wesley with helping stave off a bloody revolution, such as the one France experienced, because of the hope and spiritual revival he brought to the poor workers.

Wesley began the practice of using lay preachers – much criticized by ordained Anglican priests but a major reason Methodism spread so rapidly. And as Methodism grew, Wesley was able to fund loans for the poor, establish homes for orphans and widows, open free medical dispensaries and perform other acts of charity so deeply valued as the "the greatest of these" by Reverend Dorsey.

According to Dr. Vinson Synan, dean of the School of Divinity at Regent University in Virginia, and author of *The Holiness-Pentecostal Tradition*, John Wesley, who died in 1791, was "the spiritual and intellectual father of the modern Holiness and Pentecostal movements, which arose from Methodism in the last century."

Synan goes on to explain that Wesley's pursuit of the holiness of heart and life followed his Aldersgate spiritual awakening as a second, perfecting experience of divine grace, that became known as "sanctification," or "Christian perfection." This follows the first act of becoming a Christian through forgiveness of sins.

"At times the emotions of the sanctified Methodists would exceed the limits of control," writes Synan in his book quoting an observer. "Some would be seized with a trembling, and in a few minutes drop on the floor as if they were dead; while others were embracing each other with streaming eyes, and all were lost in wonder, love and praise."

Methodism exploded in Virginia and by 1776 that colony was home to half the Methodists in America. According to Synan, "much of drunkenness, cursing, swearing, and fighting that had characterized the colony before the 1773-76 revival gave way for a time of prayer, praise and conversing about God. This revivalistic outbreak was one of the first instances of Pentecostal-like religious revival in the nation, and was the direct antecedent of the frontier Kentucky revivals of 1800."

From their deep roots in Virginia, Methodists began sprouting growth that would eventually spread over the entire continent.

"Eighteenth-century Methodism was essentially a reaction against the prevailing creedal rigidity, liturgical strictness, and ironclan institutionalism that had largely depersonalized religion and rendered it incapable of serving the needs of individuals," writes Synan.

Methodist perfectionalism in America, similar to the Holiness movement in north Georgia, replicated Wesley's journey to a more emotional form of worship evidenced by deep feeling, outward spiritual expressions and strict morality. It was a departure from the highly centralized formal worship of the times. The growth of this "heart religion," as Wesley termed it, became a phenomenon with broad appeal to the poor and downtrodden. It also fit nicely with the optimistic spirit of hope and renewal that swept through America and its role as the "new world."

Synan cites the split over slavery and the ensuing Civil War as the causes of a major rift among Methodists north and south, which ended the quest of Holiness in the Southern churches.

"Along with the drive for perfect sanctification, there arose a parallel drive to stamp out the evil of slavery," writes Synan. "Sanctified Christians came to believe that slavery was a blot on society and the church and that it should be abolished."

In the years that followed the Civil War, controversy swirled around the pursuit of Holiness and came under attack from some of the more intellectual Methodist ministers uncomfortable with its emotionalism.

The turning point in the struggle came in 1894 at the General Conference of the Methodist Episcopal Church, South, when action was taken to end the controversy by way of a "disavowal the Holiness movement and a declaration of open warfare against its proponents."

And that, according to Synan, is when many Holiness denominations began to spring up as part of what became known as the Holiness movement. That later evolved into a still larger group known as the Pentecostal movement that had its modern day "coming out" at an explosive revival that began in 1906 at a mission located on Azusa Street in Los Angeles. Led by William Joseph Seymour, an African-American preacher, the three-and-a-half-year Azusa Street Revival was a spiritual earthquake that launched the Pentecostal movement, which spread nationwide and into the Appalachian Mountains. Seymour believed that a third spiritual blessing occurred following sanctification known as baptism of the Holy Spirit

"Sanctification cleansed and purified the believer," writes Synan. "While baptism with the Holy Spirit brought great power for service. The only biblical evidence that one had received the 'baptism' was the act of speaking in tongues as the 120 disciples had done on the day of Pentecost."

Although his humility probably would cause him to bristle at such comparisons, Reverend Dorsey has proved himself a worthy heir to Wesley, Seymour and other leaders in this "heart religion," with its anointings, sanctifications and praise spoken in many tongues. He has earned the tributes found in this book through his unwavering commitment to the verse of Corinthians he is so fond of quoting: "And now abideth faith, hope, charity, these three; but the greatest of these is charity." In the case of charity, Reverend Dorsey's cup runneth over.

Addendum, Second Edition

The Bear

This was in the late 40s. E.T. Irvin lived over at a little place called Leaf, Georgia. They had a post office over there. One morning, E.T.'s wife went out to milk at the barn. E.T. had an old sow that had little pigs. The pigs were up big enough to scamper around pretty good. While she was milking she thought it was her neighbor's black dog come and started running those pigs, and just liked to catch one.

When she got through milking she went back to the house and told E.T., "E.T., you better do something about that old black dog 'cause it just near caught one of your pigs out there."

E.T. never thought anything else about it. But it wasn't a dog, it was a black bear. The bear left E.T.'s and went on up around the back of the post office in Leaf on an old road. Some of them around the post office seen the bear, so the bear took off back up that old road into the woods. One of the owners of the store there at Leaf was Mr. Kenimer. Mr. Kenimer's oldest son, Jones, grabbed a shotgun, and he and another fella went up the road the way the bear went.

My neighbor called me and said, "Get over here quick with your rifle, there's a bear out!" I had a 16-shot Remington automatic rifle.

This is when bears were first turned loose in the mountains and of course it was against the law to kill one. But we forgot about that. I jumped in my car with my rifle to run over there. Wiley Barrett, a man that lived just above there, he met me at the store and we went up the old road. Jones and man that went with him were standing up there next to an old brush pile. They told us that when they got up there they stopped and looked around and Jones put his foot up on the side of the brush pile. When he did, the brush pile just raised up and that bear come out. Jones throwed up his hands and hollered, "Help! Help!" He forgot to even shoot at the bear.

The bear went on down through the woods. We got up there and they told us the way he went so we went in that direction – two or three hundred yards down through the woods. And there the bear set up in a tree. We shot him and he come tumbling down.

By that time several men had gathered and they was wondering what they was going to do with the bear. Some of them said Mr. Anderson has a meat market over in Clarkesville, let's just take him over there and get him to dress the bear for eatin'. So they went and got a pickup and loaded him on the pickup and carried him over to Mr. Anderson's. I wasn't with them when they went to Mr. Anderson's, but they told him they had a bear they wanted dressed and cut up in packages.

Mr. Anderson said, "Boys, I'll make a deal with you. I'll dress the bear and cut him up in packages for the hide."

That was a good deal for the boys. When they got the bear packaged they brought all that bear meat and put in a freezer locker I had on my back porch. My wife cooked a mess of it up and the longer I chewed that bear meat, the bigger it got. So we didn't try no more of it. We had a neighbor that had a big family and they were sort of up against it. They started eating on that bear meat and they eat every bit of it.

The game warden heard about us killing a bear so he come down to Leaf and inquired about it. They told the game warden, "Yes, they carried the bear over to Anderson's meat market in Clarkesville."

So the game warden went over there and asked Mr. Anderson about it.

Mr. Anderson said, "Yeah, I dressed the bear and packaged him. That bear was over there at Leaf trying to break in the post office so they shot him."

The game warden, knowing it was a federal offense to break in a post office, he just turned around and left.

Afterword by Candice Dyer

On a fitful night in the '60s, Rev. Asa Dorsey, a Holiness preacher in the hills of north Georgia, experienced a strange dream.

"My brother and I were bass fishing in the dream," he says. "We felt a tug on the line and struggled with it, thinking it was the biggest fish we'd ever caught. It turned out to be a young man with long hair."

In a vision that would prove prophetic, the Dorsey brothers had reeled in a hippie.

Soon afterward, Rev. Dorsey's country church attracted a contingent of flower children whose grooming habits and shagadelic lingo – calling the ladies "chicks" for example – rattled the locals.

"In the dream, I was taking extra care to clean the minnows we were using as bait," Rev. Dorsey says. "And when those hippies arrived in their raggedy clothes, they sure did need some cleaning up. But I never preached against their long hair or the way they smelled."

As a result, the hippies embraced both hygiene and the gospel. Four of them became ministers.

As he shares this bit of sociological testimony, Rev. Dorsey, now 87, is not leaning on a pulpit, but he definitely has the floor.

He has enjoyed many "anointings," and one of them is a gift for telling stories. They tumble out, as natural and irrepressible as a highland creek, funny ones and poignant ones, all of them glinting with truth and timed just right. He speaks with an elocution and vocabulary which belie a formal education that ended in grade school. Like a waterfall discovered in a quiet recess of the woods, his words seem to originate from some serene, pristine place.

If you are in his company, your first instinct is to hush, not because he speechifies like a loud-mouthed showboat but because he does just the opposite. Rev. Dorsey is an unusually soft-spoken, modest man, a sympathetic listener rather than a conversation-hog. Still, sitting here in his living room – wherever two or more are gathered, as the saying goes – he just can't help riveting his listeners.

Out of the blue, he tells me: "I learned early on, when I was a child, not to feel prejudice toward black people. I remember a little black boy my grandfather took in to raise. One evening he offered me a ride on a bay horse, and put my arms around him and rode. From that day one, I knew not to feel prejudice. I've always thought a lot of black people."

He pauses, thinking back.

"Some of the black men I worked with on a farm wanted me to preach to their church," he says. "When I went to meet with them, I saw that for a pulpit, they had put a sheet over a chair for me. That was fine and good. …But I'd have felt a lot better without that sheet!"

His round, Celtic face crinkles into a grin.

Then the subject turns to his late wife, Annie Kate, the sweet-natured soul-mate who is never far from his thoughts.

"She was the epitome of patience," he says. "I needed her so much. We didn't have marriage counseling in those days, but we learned a whole heap from experience."

Rev. Dorsey has stored up a vast reserve of insights from his calling – praying at deathbeds, dunking the newly saved backward into the tonic waters of a chilly lake, conferring with everyone from angels to plain-folk at their most fallible – but he wears his wisdom as lightly as a Sunday hat. He is what people mean when they say "salt of the earth," and I think of him as one big beatitude in the compact form of a country gentleman.

I grew up in near Rev. Dorsey and graduated from high school with two of his grandchildren. He knew my family members and their chicken farms through his poultry-inspection work. Whenever Rev. Dorsey's name came up in conversation, someone inevitably would remark, "He's one fine fella." Then another would relate a tale that illustrated Rev. Dorsey's generosity.

Still, I had never heard him preach.

As a young reporter for *The Telegraph* in 1990, I was assigned to write an article about the commemoration of Rev. Dorsey's 57th year in the ministry. I am embarrassed to admit that, during that time when I was drifting away from the church, I was expecting a doctrinaire sermon that would make my eyes glaze over. Instead, I was inspired by observations that were both whimsical and profound as he explained his "happiness philosophy."

Here is one of his quotations from the resulting article:

"In counseling, I coined a word for happiness: mip. If your motive is seeking happiness you'll never find it because happiness is a shy little mip that stays just a few steps ahead of you. But when you forget about yourself and help others, the shy mip comes to you. The greatest happiness of all is making others happy. It's a lasting virtue."

Rev. Dorsey must be tending a whole herd of mips by now.

Today, in his dress suspenders and a starchy white shirt with a gold fountain pen gleaming in his pocket, Rev. Dorsey looks like a dapper squire. His parents named him after Asa Candler, the Coca-Cola magnate and symbol of old-money Atlanta.

However, Rev. Dorsey, called "Asie" by his friends, pursued a different fortune as one of the Southeast's most esteemed evangelists. His interpretation of scripture, which he quotes from memory with crackerjack accuracy, emphasizes charity over the single-minded pursuit of wealth.

"Real charity is giving the last that we got," he says in *The Greatest of These*. "That was the widow's mites. ...This doctrine of God giving you riches – and I've heard preachers say that the blessings of God means there should be a Cadillac in every garage – is not backed up by the Bible. Jesus never had anything to ride on until he made his entrance into Jerusalem, and he borrowed a colt to do that."

No adherent of the fashionable "prosperity theology," Rev. Dorsey would rather give away his possessions than acquire more. He has been the shadowy figure leaving bags of groceries on a hungry family's doorstep or secretly paying off a friend's debts. To the consternation of local bureaucrats, he even requested to pay more taxes to ensure that his bill would be equivalent with his neighbor's. So it seems only natural to draw the title of his memoir from one of his favorite Bible verses: "And now abideth faith, hope, charity, these three; but the greatest of these is charity."

All of these values shine through the recollections in this book. Country preachers often are perceived as dogmatic enforcers, inclined more toward brimstone-spiked admonitions than open-hearted understanding. These musings by Rev. Dorsey, however, bear witness to the agape of Christianity that sustains as it mysti-fies: We are flawed and our lives troubled, but Jesus will help us do better – and he expects us to help each other. With his gentle delivery and nonjudgmental sensibility, Rev. Dorsey demonstrates that old-time religion does not have to breathe fire and pound the pulpit; it can land as softly as a dove.

At his altar, all have been welcome – struggling farmers, shaggy hippies and at least one cantankerous billy goat. He has seen way-ward husbands give up hooch and bonnet-topped grannies renounce snuff. Several lovestruck couples have sought his services for impromptu, creek-bank weddings, and they credit the longevity of their unions to his blessing.

Still, Rev. Dorsey is best known for his soothing eulogies at funerals. His kindly manner and personal touch with the telling anecdote (in most cases, he could trace the genealogy of the deceased through several generations) are legendary for the com-fort they have brought grieving loved ones. Toting up more than 1,700 services, he is believed to hold a regional record for officiat-ing at the most funerals.

Rev. Dorsey also is a master of preacherly politesse. Suppose two ministers were planning to read the same passage at a service? No matter. Rev. Dorsey stores enough verses in his memory's data-base to choose another chapter and launch into a celestial riff with-out pausing to wipe his brow. Like many Appalachian word-lovers who grew up too poor to own a library, Rev. Dorsey memorized whatever he could get his work-callused hands on. "If I got it memorized, and they took the Bible from me, they couldn't take it out of my mind," he has said.

Still, Rev. Dorsey's remarkable gifts were not always well-received. This memoir sheds light on the underreported hostility and, in some cases, outright persecution that often greeted the Holiness movement in North Georgia. When folks from other denominations threw rocks at his tents, Rev. Dorsey, in a Christ-like gesture, simply invited his attackers to the altar. I am proud to note that my great-grandmother, Ollie Jarrard, a hard-shell Baptist, was one of the locals who embraced Rev. Dorsey. He officiated at her funeral.

Rev. Dorsey's memories of the Depression, farming, sawmilling, old childhood games, family rituals and the rigors of a sacred calling also provide a glimpse of mountain life in a time when people derived a sense of community from log-raisings and tent revivals rather than chat rooms.

It all makes for an inheritance more lucrative than any Coca-Cola stock portfolio.

"As I sit here thinking back over my life of 87 years," Rev. Dorsey says. "It's been a wonderful experience, and surely I'm the richest man in the world, not in bank accounts, bonds and dollars and cents, but that's not where true riches lie. I'm an heir to the Kingdom of God with Jesus Christ. What greater riches could you obtain?

Author Larry Fricks, with Grace and four footeds (l-r) Squeaky the cat, and dogs Zeus and Blue, at home in Turner's Corner.

Larry Fricks has a journalism degree from the University of Georgia and served as a staff writer and columnist for the *The Telegraph* in Cleveland and *The Times* in Gainesville. He co-authored a book titled *Mountain Lines* named for his weekly columns in *The Times*. Larry has published stories in the *Georgia Journal* and *Georgia Living* and has won journalism awards from the Associated Press, the Georgia Press Association and Gannett Newspapers, He resides with his wife, Grace, in the north Lumpkin County community of Turner's Corner.